To our son, Franklin Jay.
May you take after your wonderful mother
and always shoot for eagles and birdies
in a world of pars and bogies.

GOLF SHORTS

1,001 OF THE GAME'S FUNNIEST ONE-LINERS

GLENN LIEBMAN

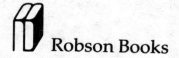

Robson Books

First published in Great Britain in 1995 by Robson Books Ltd, Bolsover
House, 5-6 Clipstone Street, London W1P 8LE

Copyright © 1995 Glenn Liebman
The right of Glenn Liebman to be identified as author of this work has
been asserted by him in accordance with the Copyright, Designs and
Patents Act 1988

British Library Cataloguing in Publication Data
A catalogue record for this title is available from the British Library

ISBN 1 86105 012 7

Printed in Great Britain by Biddles Ltd, Guildford and King's Lynn

ACKNOWLEDGMENTS

First of all, thanks to the hilarious characters of golf who made this book possible.

I would like to thank my agent extraordinaire, Philip Spitzer, and the people at Contemporary—especially my wonderful editor, Nancy Crossman, the marketing expert behind the Shorts series; Publisher Christine Albritton, who came up with the idea for a golf book; Maureen Musker, the publicist who responds professionally and with good humor to my frequently inane questions; and Project Editor Craig Bolt, who helps make these one-liners come to life and who will be most likely to jump off the roof when the White Sox trade Frank Thomas for Todd Hundley. (Hey, I can dream, can't I?)

I am eternally grateful to my late mother, Frieda, for nurturing my love of sports. How many other mothers would negotiate with scalpers to get tickets for my brother and me for the 1973 NBA Playoffs or urge me not to throw out all my baseball cards (which I did anyway during a brief neatness phase of my life)? Thanks also to my father, Bernie, who has given me enthusiastic support and encouragement throughout my writing career. I owe a great deal to my in-laws, Bill and Helen Coll, who do so much for us and ask so little in return.

The two people to whom I owe the biggest debt of gratitude are my brother, Bennett, and my wife, Kathy. Over the last thirty-six years, my brother has been my confidant, my sounding board, my friend, the father of two of the cutest girls in history, and the only person with whom I can talk sports for twenty-four hours a day, seven days a week.

Despite a difficult pregnancy, my wife has put up with my long hours and obsession with golf one-liners with grace and good humor—even though she doesn't know the difference between Arnold Palmer and Arnold Horshack. She continues to be my greatest source of strength.

INTRODUCTION

In 1967, when I was ten years old, my mother took my brother and me to our first golf tournament—a practice round for the U.S. Open. I had a great time running around with my little autograph pad: Billy Casper gave me a great big smile and spent a few minutes chatting with me, Julius Boros willingly signed my notepad, and the Golden Bear himself patted me on the head. That small display of affection turned my mother into Nicklaus's biggest fan for the next twenty years.

When we got home, my father quizzed my brother and me about who our favorite players were. Giving it about as much thought as a ten-year-old gives to anything, I immediately shouted "Don Bies" because he was friendly to me and had a great name.

My brother, who was older and vastly more knowledgeable about golf, said he was very impressed with the play of a young guy named Lee something or other. I laughed and told him that Don Bies would be the greatest player of all time and Lee what's-his-name would never be heard from again.

Today, twenty-seven years later, my brother still reminds me about that prediction. In fact, every sports prediction I make is measured against the Don Bies–Lee Trevino argument. It makes no difference that my brother said Ralph Sampson would be better than Kareem or that Eric Davis was better than Willie Mays. He will always be one up on me because of Bies-Trevino.

Despite the years of harassment, I am glad my brother was correct in his assessment. Trevino's rise to prominence has been a boon to those of us who write sports humor books. He is undoubtedly the funniest man in all of sports: For example, asked his reasons for joining the Senior Tour, he replied, "Why play with the flat bellies when you can play with the round bellies?" In response to a comment about his wild spending habits, he once said, "I never saw a Brinks truck following a funeral procession." After seeing three partners hit balls into the woods, Trevino asked, "What's over there, a nudist camp?"

When I started working on this book, I was familiar with some of Trevino's great quotes and those of other notable golf humorists: Chi Chi Rodriguez (on reaching a million dollars in career earnings—"The problem is, I'm already over $2 million in spending"), Bob Hope (on playing golf with George Meaney—"He plays just like a union man. He negotiates the final score"), and television analyst Gary McCord (on comparisons between himself and Bob Uecker—"The difference is Uecker only played baseball for about five years. I've been dismal at golf for 17 or 18"). But I was amazed to discover the countless other golfers over the years who have injected so much humor into this wonderful game: old-time greats like Jimmy Demaret (who advised a struggling golfer to "take two weeks off and then quit the game") and Lloyd Mangrum (asked if he was interested in writing a book, he replied, "Are you kidding? The only big word I know is delicatessen; and I can't even spell it"), current stars like Peter Jacobsen (on the difference between the pros and amateurs— "When a pro hits it to the right, it's called a fade. When an amateur hits it, it's called a slice") and Nick Faldo (on his marriage—"We were happily married for eight months. Unfortunately, we were married for four and a half years"), and Senior Tour veterans like Bob Bruce ("You know you're getting old when your back goes out more than you do") and Roger Maltbie (asked what he would have to shoot to win a tournament, he said, "The rest of the field").

Whether you are a member of Arnie's Army or Dean's Drunks (as Dean Martin called his followers), there is something here for every golf fan. So sit back, relax, and enjoy the funniest lines of this grand game.

P.S.: Regretfully, there are no great lines from Don Bies in this book, but please don't tell my brother.

"The most abysmal advice ever given by the ignorant to the stupid."

Tommy Armour, on keeping your eye on the ball

"Why don't you aim more to the right?"

Ben Hogan, to a player asking for advice on why he always hits his shots to the left

"If you can get the ball in the hole regularly by standing on your head, then keep right on—and don't ever listen to advice from anyone."

John Jacobs, British golf teacher

"Never give a golfer an ultimatum unless you're prepared to lose."

Abigail Van Buren ("Dear Abby")

"Years ago we discovered the exact point, the dead center of middle age. It occurs when you are too young to take up golf and too old to rush to the net."

Franklin Adams, American journalist

"That's the easiest 69 I ever made."

Walter Hagen, on turning 69

"You know you're getting old when all the names in your black book have M.D. after them."

Arnold Palmer

"I'm getting so old, I don't even buy green bananas anymore."

Chi Chi Rodriguez

"Once a guy gets past 50, if he misses one day of playing, he goes back two."

Sam Snead

"The road's getting shorter and narrower, but I'll play wherever the pigeons land."

Sam Snead, at age 81

"His nerve, his memory, and I can't remember the third thing."

> Lee Trevino, on the three things an aging golfer loses

"When the big four-oh jumps up and grabs you, you realize there's only a limited amount of time left. It brings a sense of urgency."

> Lanny Wadkins, on winning two tournaments at age 40

"What do I do better now? Probably sleep."

> Larry Ziegler, when asked what he does better now than he did 20 years ago

AGENTS

"He put his arm around me and said, 'Palsy-walsy, you and I are going to make a lot of money.' I've steered clear of agents since."

> Bob Goalby

"I'm about as concerned as Jack would be if he read that I was practicing to compete in the Masters."

> *Mark McCormack, superagent and owner of a sports management firm, on Jack Nicklaus's new sports management firm*

"I've never met one. I guess they're a different type of critter."

> *Tom Wargo, on agents*

AMATEURS

"Had you ever thought of playing the Tour? You could give everyone lessons on how to starve to death."

> *Furman Bisher, sportswriter, on what golfers really think when they make encouraging remarks to amateurs*

"The amateur has an infectious, contagious enthusiasm for golf and life."

> *Mac O'Grady*

"I told him he was one year away from the Tour and next year he'll be two years away."

Chi Chi Rodriguez, on the potential of an amateur

"I like the thought of playing for money instead of silverware. I never did like to polish."

Patty Sheehan, on turning pro

"It keeps guys like Jack Lemmon from making an 8 or a 9 on national television."

Fuzzy Zoeller, on the idea of moving tees up for amateurs in celebrity tournaments

AN-TEE SOCIAL

"I don't answer the phone. I get the feeling whenever I do that there will be someone on the other end."

Fred Couples

"Golf isn't like other sports where you can take a player out if he's having a bad day. You have to play the whole game."

> *Phil Blackmar, on a third-round 78 that cost him a tournament*

"I lost that round in a bar."

> *Roger Maltbie, on shooting a record 92 at a tournament after going out drinking the night before*

"If I had been in the gallery, I'd have gone home."

> *Johnny Miller, on shooting a 39 on the first nine holes of a tournament*

"I feel like I've been beaten up by the neighborhood bully."

> *Mac O'Grady, after a bad round*

"That round of golf was like a first date. She didn't care for me and I didn't like her. I tried to kiss her, but she slapped me. I was afraid to come back for a second date."

> *Mac O'Grady, on withdrawing from an event after shooting a 79 on the first round*

"I think I'll go to Hertz and see if I can rent a game."

> *Phil Rodgers, after a bad round*

SEVE BALLESTEROS

"All of a sudden I had friends I hadn't seen or heard from in years. And, oddly enough, they all had daughters and just wanted to drop by my house."

> *Bynna Barner, wife of Ballesteros's agent, on having the golfer over for lunch*

"God said to Faldo, as He once said to Nicklaus, 'You will have skills like no other.' Then He whispered to Ballesteros, as He whispered to Palmer, 'but they will love you more.'"

> *Tom Callahan, columnist for the Washington Post*

7

"Seve can have an off week and still win. But if Seve plays well and the rest of us play well, Seve wins."
Ben Crenshaw

"He goes after a golf course like a lion at a zebra. He doesn't reason with it. . . . He tries to hold its head under the water until it stops wriggling."
Jim Murray

MILLER BARBER

"He looks like somebody's always chasing him."
Gary McCord, on Barber's disheveled appearance

"I envy that man. Because he makes a hundred thousand dollars a year like I do, but nobody knows him."
Mickey Mantle

DEANE BEMAN

"He's just another screwhead too big for his britches."
Bill Murray

"He must have no nerves at all."
Jack Nicklaus, on Beman's putting skills

BEST AND BRIGHTEST

"I'm the best. I just haven't played yet."
Muhammad Ali, on golf

"Imagine what golf has done for a dumb guy like me."
George Archer, on making millions from playing the game

"I owe everything to golf. Where else could a guy with an IQ like mine make this much money?"
Hubert Green

"I try to be semi-humble. If I started going around saying how good I was, everything would go wrong."

Johnny Miller

"Nobody ever heard Jack Nicklaus say 'I don't know.' About anything."

Johnny Miller

"When you're playing well, you can hit the ball within a foot of where you want it to land."

Greg Norman

"You know me. If you hear me tell you a mosquito can pull a wagon, you better hitch it up, son."

Jerry Pate

"I never exaggerate. I just remember big."

Chi Chi Rodriguez

"If it wasn't for golf, I don't know what I'd be doing. If my IQ had been two points lower, I'd have been a plant somewhere."

Lee Trevino

"I know I had a couple of drinks last night, but I didn't expect to wake up in Sun Valley, Idaho."

> *Jimmy Demaret, on partying the night before a fluke snowstorm at the Crosby Pro-Am in Monterey, California*

"I'm going to be around until the Atomic Energy Commission finds a safe place to bury my liver."

> *Phil Harris, on how long he will continue to golf*

"Michelob when the sun is up and Scotch when the sun goes down."

> *Roger Maltbie, on his choice of drinks*

"You've heard of Arnie's Army. Well, those are Dean's Drunks."

> *Dean Martin, on his followers on the golf course*

"If you drive, don't drink. Don't even putt."

> *Dean Martin*

"It'll be nice not to use my fake IDs anymore."
Phil Mickelson, on turning 21

"It could be worse; I could be allergic to beer."
Greg Norman, on being allergic to grass

"The first time I played the Masters, I was so nervous I drank a bottle of rum before I teed off. I shot the happiest 83 of my life."
Chi Chi Rodriguez

"It tasted a little chemical at first."
Patty Sheehan, on drinking from the LPGA Trophy after winning the 1993 Championship

"My friend Tom Purtzer says I just eat it so I have an excuse to drink margaritas."
Howard Twitty, on his love of Mexican food

"Moderation is essential in all things, madam, but never in my life have I failed to beat a teetotaler."
Harry Vardon, on being asked to join the temperance movement

"I tried to make a one, but I made two of them instead."

Al Kelley, Senior Tour Golfer, on getting an 11 on a par-5 hole

"It's like a cold slap in the face. You're mad and you're not trying to protect anything out there anymore."

Mark McCumber, on the effects of a quadruple bogey

"Easy. I missed a 20-footer for a 12."

Arnold Palmer, on being asked how he could possibly shoot a 13 on a hole

TOMMY BOLT

"If Bolt had a head on his shoulders, he would have been the best golfer who ever lived."

Ben Hogan, on the terrible temper of Tommy Bolt

JULIUS BOROS

"He's Perry Como's kid by another marriage."
> *Don Rickles, on the laid-back play of*
> *Boros*

BRITISH OPEN

"A championship course is not a championship course until a championship has been played upon it."
> *Michael Bonallack, Secretary of the*
> *Royal and Ancient Golf Club of St.*
> *Andrews*

"How's my name going to fit on that thing?"
> *Mark Calcavecchia, on the trophy*
> *awarded him for winning the 1989*
> *British Open*

"The reason the Road Hole is the greatest par 4 in the world is because it's a par 5."
> *Ben Crenshaw, on the 17th hole at St.*
> *Andrews*

"You can play a damned good shot and find the ball in a damned bad place."

George Duncan, on St. Andrews

"They are the same people who knock the pyramids because they don't have elevators."

Jim Ferree, on players who complain about St. Andrews

"There's nothing wrong with the St. Andrews course that 100 bulldozers couldn't put right. The Old Course needs a dry clean and press."

Ed Furjol, Senior Tour golfer

"It's so calm, even the golfers are disappointed. It's the British Open, and I expect wind. It just doesn't make me feel like I'm playing the British Open."

Hubert Green

"He must have left a hole out."

Hale Irwin, on Seve Ballesteros shooting a 16 in the last five holes of the 1979 British Open at Royal Lytham and St. Annes

"The more I studied the Old Course, the more I loved it; and the more I loved it, the more I studied it."

Bobby Jones, on St. Andrews

"When the British Open is in Scotland, there's something special about it. And when it's at St. Andrews, it's even greater."

Jack Nicklaus

"I wish I had kept my damn mouth shut."

Jack Nicklaus, after he gave Lee Trevino encouragement and Trevino ended up beating him at the 1971 Open

"If you're going to be a player people will remember, you have to win the Open at St. Andrews."

Jack Nicklaus

"Nick Faldo's victory in the British Open earned him another green jacket."

Dan Patrick, ESPN commentator, confusing the majors

"**M**aybe we Americans should come and look at this course, considering the crap we are building today."

Curtis Strange, on St. Andrews

"**H**ow can they beat me? I've been struck by lightning, had two back operations, and been divorced twice."

Lee Trevino, on his prospects for winning the 1983 British Open

"**A**t 15 we put down my bag to hunt for a ball, found the ball, lost the bag."

Lee Trevino, at Royal Birkdale

"**W**hat if Isao Aoki had won?"

Lee Trevino, told by a cabdriver that he named his child after whoever won the 1972 British Open, won by Trevino

"**O**nly Opens."

Tom Watson, asked if he collected anything Scottish for good luck

"The only equivalent plunge from genius I could think of was Ernest Hemingway's tragic loss of ability to write. Hemingway got up one morning and shot himself. Nicklaus got up the next morning and shot 66."

> *Ian Wooldridge, British journalist, on Nicklaus shooting 83 in the first round of the British Open and following that up with a 66*

BUNKERS

"Make them tee it up in the Open left-handed. Put 40,000 people out there watching them play from the other side. Let Nicklaus, Kite, Watson, and Floyd get in a bunker and try to get out left-handed. Everybody would be giggling and laughing."

> *Mac O'Grady, on what he would do to spice up the game*

"If your opponent is playing several shots in vain attempts to extricate himself from a bunker, do not stand near him and audibly count his strokes. It would be justifiable homicide if he wound up his pitiable exhibition by applying his niblick to your head."

> *Harry Vardon*

"I wasn't even on the Top 60 in caddie earnings before the Kemper."

> *J. C. Anderson, touring pro, on getting $46,000 for finishing 6th at the Kemper Open*

"If it weren't for golf, I'd probably be a caddie today."
> *George Archer*

"He told me he caddied in the same group with me in the Hot Springs Open. That's why I voted for him, because he was a caddie."
> *Tommy Bolt, on Bill Clinton*

"Get home? I don't even know where you live."
> *Jackie Burke's caddie, after Burke asked him how to get home from the green*

"I couldn't figure it out. I wore deodorant and everything."
> *Marlene Hagge, on having five caddies in one day at a tournament*

"If I needed advice from my caddie, he'd be hitting the shots and I'd be carrying the bag."

> *Bobby Jones, asked how dependent he was on advice from his caddie*

"She knows how to hang on to her money. I wish her mom were the same way."

> *Orville Moody, on having his daughter caddie for him*

"Do I ever disagree with him on course strategy? Never—unless he's wrong."

> *Gary Nicklaus, on caddying for his father*

"Never pick up a lost golf ball while it's still rolling."

> *Jack Nicklaus, asked what advice he gives to caddies*

"Essentially, he has been retired since he was 21."

> *Jack Nicklaus, on the work habits of his longtime caddie Angelo Argea*

"When I caddied there, I was paid 10 cents a bag. And if you lost a ball, they kicked your butt and fired you. I never lost a ball."

> *Chi Chi Rodriguez, on caddying as a child in Puerto Rico*

"You ought to be a singer, man, because you got legs like a canary."

> *Chi Chi Rodriguez, to his caddie, who was dressed in knickers and knee socks*

"He told me just to keep the ball low."

> *Chi Chi Rodriguez, on the advice his caddie gave him on a crucial putt*

"It's kind of like the millionaire who goes down to skid row and hangs around to see what's going on."

> *J. C. Snead, on Dwayne Morrison leaving his job as basketball coach at Georgia Tech to be Snead's caddie*

"Nobody but you and your caddie care what you do out there, and if your caddie is betting against you, he doesn't care, either."

> *Lee Trevino*

"Well, sir, I'd recommend the 4:05 train."

> *Harry Vardon's caddie, after Vardon asked him, "What should I take here?"*

MARK CALCAVECCHIA

"For the first time I felt like they used to feel when they played with me—Mark hits it so hard and far, I felt totally inadequate."

> *Jack Nicklaus*

BILLY CASPER

"I really don't know if there ever was a Big Three [Nicklaus, Palmer, and Player] in professional golf. If there was, it should have been a Big Four, with Billy Casper in there. There's no way you could leave Casper out."

> *Orville Moody*

"Most of these guys only want to grow up and mature. When I retire, I'm going to enjoy being a black multi-millionaire."

> *Charles Barkley, on the celebrity golf tour*

"On one hole I'm like Arnold Palmer, and on the next like Lilli Palmer."

> *Sean Connery*

"I'm actually a little nervous, like it's my first pro tournament. The first swing might be a little scary."

> *Jimmy Connors, on playing at the Pebble Beach Pro-Am*

"I really like Bill, but I don't think I'd ever go down to a set where he's shooting a movie and jump and scream like a maniac."

> *Fred Couples, on the antics of Bill Murray at the Pebble Beach Pro-Am*

"That's Jack Benny. He's always out there on bad days like that looking for golf balls."

> Bing Crosby, after a skin diver came out of the water at the 16th hole of the Crosby Pro-Am

"All tennis courts look alike."

> Bradford Dillman, actor, on why he likes golf more than tennis

"The safest place would be in the fairway."

> Joe Garagiola, on the best place for spectators to stand during celebrity golf tournaments

"You've got to be rich to have a swing like that."

> Bob Hope, on the elegant swing of Bing Crosby

"He hits the ball 130 yards and his jewelry goes 150."

> Bob Hope, on the golf game of Sammy Davis, Jr.

"If you think it's hard to meet new people, try picking up the wrong golf ball."

> Jack Lemmon

"Forward the check to charity to help offset the cost of all the condo windows I broke during my play here."

Gary McCord, on winning $2,000 at the Bob Hope Open

"I can't hit a ball more than 200 yards. I have no butt. You need a butt if you're going to hit a golf ball."

Dennis Quaid, on losing weight for a movie

"He'd be in sneakers and wearing a dirty sweatshirt, and when we finished, he'd take me to the grubbiest, most awful restaurant you can imagine."

Gene Sarazen, on playing golf with Howard Hughes

"If you call personality the battle of Hollywood stars, then yes, we do lack personality. But the personality of golf is good golf. If you want to see a comedian, you ought to tune in Saturday Night Live."

Tom Watson, criticizing those who say that golf lacks celebrities

CHEATING

"Most people play a fair game of golf—if you watch them."

Joey Adams

"If there is any larceny in a man, golf will bring it out."

Paul Gallico

"Isn't it fun to go out on the course and lie in the sun?"

Bob Hope

"He plays just like a union man. He negotiates the final score."

Bob Hope, on playing golf with George Meany

"I have a tip that can take five strokes off anyone's golf game. It's called an eraser."

Arnold Palmer

"It taught me perseverance, it taught me not to cheat—no easy thing for a boy when he's two down and his ball is deep in the woods."

James Reston, on the lessons of golf

"The income tax has made more liars out of the American people than golf has."

Will Rogers

"Golf is a game in which the ball lies poorly and the players well."

Art Rosenbaum

CHIP SHOTS

"I tell 'em to take 100 chip shots and when they make 100 in a row, we go on to putting."

Jackie Burke, on giving golf lessons

"The first one was okay. The second one was pretty tough."

Gene Sauers, after John Cook chipped in two straight playoff holes to beat Sauers

CHOKE HOLD

"They keep trying to give me a championship, but I won't take it."

> *Leo Diegel, on choking in the last*
> *round of the 1933 British Open*

"Absolutely everyone has done it, but there are few people who admit it."

> *David Feherty, on choking*

"Everyone has his own choking level, a level at which he fails to play his normal golf. As you get more experienced, your choking level rises."

> *Johnny Miller*

"You can video your swing all you want, but when old Joe Choke grabs you around the throat, that guy's video is not going to be there to help you."

> *Lee Trevino*

"Flippy-wristed little college kids."

> *Tommy Bolt, on young players against whom he competed*

"Betsy studied and played golf. I played golf, partied, and studied a little."

> *Beth Daniel, on being a college teammate of Betsy King*

"Five minutes at the school."

> *John Huston, on spending two semesters on the golf team at Auburn*

"I wasn't there long enough to hear them say what they were."

> *John Huston, on the courses he took at Auburn*

"I probably would have taken it. Except they wanted me to rent cross-country skis during the winter."

> *Tom Lehman, on being offered the job as golf coach at the University of Minnesota*

"I kinda screwed up my redshirt year, then had to take incompletes in summer school because I went golfing every day."

> *Jim McMahon, NFL quarterback, on not graduating from Brigham Young in four years*

"I thought all the guys who played golf were a bunch of sissies. They all wore pink sweaters."

> *Larry Nelson, on why he played basketball and football in school instead of golf*

COMPANIONSHIP

"Golf is like fishing and hunting. What counts is the companionship and fellowship of friends, not what you catch or shoot."

> *George Archer*

"Golf is the only sport that a professional can enjoy playing with his friends. Can Larry Holmes enjoy fighting one of his friends?"

> *Chi Chi Rodriguez*

"If you guarantee them $20,000 for second place, they wouldn't take it. They must have the opportunity to win. If I were offered the same money, I'd grab it and stay home and watch the tournament on TV."

Frank Beard, 1970, on the obsession with winning of several players

"How would you like to meet the top 143 people at what you do each week in order to survive?"

Bruce Crampton

"I play with friends sometimes, but there are never friendly games."

Ben Hogan

"There are always some fellows in there against you, shooting just as good golf or better."

Ben Hogan, on what drove him to be the best

"On tour we get paid for performance. If we don't play well, our income falls dramatically. If we get hurt and have to sit out a season, there's no income at all."

Tom Kite

"The rest of the field."

> *Roger Maltbie, asked what he had to shoot to win a tournament*

"Still your shot."

> *Dave Marr, on the three ugliest words in golf*

"Three holes to go and you need two pars and a birdie to win."

> *Jack Nicklaus, asked about his most exciting prospect in golf*

"I always look to see what Arnold shot; it's a habit. We will always compete against each other."

> *Jack Nicklaus*

"Eighteen holes of match or medal play will teach you more about your foe than will 18 years of dealing with him across a desk."

> *Grantland Rice, famed sportswriter*

"I've had dinner with three players in 14 years out here. I don't want to get to know these guys. With nine holes to play, I want them to worry about not knowing me."

Lee Trevino

CONDITIONING

"I used golf as a Zen exercise. . . . I learned that a person who is able to concentrate and focus can do almost anything."

T Bone Burnett, rock musician

"Exercise will build up your body, but it won't do your score any good."

Bobby Nichols

FRED COUPLES

"He's a threat to win until his brain turns into tapioca."

Gary McCord

"What I want is Fred Couples's face. And I want Fred Couples's body. And Fred Couples's swing. His hair . . . I want anybody's hair."

Rocky Thompson, Senior Tour pro

COURSES

"They don't build courses for people. They build monuments to themselves."

George Archer, on golf architects

"There's something haunting about getting up at dawn and walking a golf course, checking pin placements. It's easy to lose track of reality."

Ernest "Creamy" Carolan, longtime caddie for many stars, including Arnold Palmer and Ben Hogan

"Golf is not a fair game, so why build a course fair?"

Pete Dye, golf architect

"I'd rather be on a golf course than eat. If I couldn't go and dig some dirt, you might as well put me in a box."

Pete Dye

"I like going there for golf. America's one vast golf course today."

Edward, Duke of Windsor

"It's not like something from Ireland or Scotland. It's like something from Mars."

David Feherty, on the Ocean Course at Kiawah Island

"This place is like one of those hot-air hand dryers in toilets. It's a great idea and everybody uses it once, but never again. It takes too long."

David Feherty, on a golf course designed by Jack Nicklaus in Grand Cypress, Florida

"Golf courses are like children. I have no favorites."

Robert Trent Jones, famed golf designer

"Every hole should be a difficult par and a comfortable bogey."

Robert Trent Jones

"It's like replacing Bo Derek with Roseanne Barr."
> *Johnny Miller, on Poppy Hills replacing Cypress Point as the home for the AT&T Pro-Am*

"I want to win here, stand on the 18th green, and say 'I'm going to the World Series.' "
> *Larry Nelson, on a golf tournament in Disney World*

"Trent Jones must have laid this one out in a kennel."
> *Bob Rosburg, on all the doglegs at the Hazeltine, Minnesota, golf course*

"Trent Jones must have a permanent crick in his neck. Every time he walks down a fairway, he's looking behind him to see how he can make the hole longer."
> *Gene Sarazen*

"Some of us worship in churches, some in synagogues, some on golf courses."
> *Adlai Stevenson*

"Even the men's room has a double dogleg."
> *Dave Stockton, on the Poppy Hills course in Pebble Beach*

"His courses are like Jack himself: grim and humorless, with sharp edges."

> *Peter Thomson, on golf courses designed by Jack Nicklaus*

BEN CRENSHAW

"The kid draws people. You could send him out in the middle of the desert with a sand wedge, and all of a sudden there'd be 10,000 fans around him."

> *John Schlee, on the early career of Ben Crenshaw*

JOHN DALY

"His driving is unbelievable. I don't go that far on my holidays."

> *Ian Baker-Finch*

"John certainly gives it a good hit, doesn't he? My Sunday best is a Wednesday afternoon compared to him."

> *Nick Faldo*

"He is just ridiculous with his length. I couldn't hit it where he hits it on a runway."
Fred Funk

"Did you know John Daly hit a tee shot—and two tracking stations picked it up as a satellite?"
Jim Murray

"John Daly's in another league. Now that I'm qualified for another league myself, maybe I should stay there."
Jack Nicklaus, referring to the Senior Tour

"Nobody cares if John Daly shoots 80. They just want to see him hit a ball."
Gene Sarazen

"I just kept wanting to see him take a belt at it. It was like watching a singer or somebody who makes your hair come up on your neck."
Sam Snead

"My caddie dared me to try it, but I don't think it was worth losing a ball."
Ian Woosnam, after Daly hit a 421-yard shot

"If she used a driver off the tee and kept it in the fairway—the rest of us would be playing for second most of the time."

> *Nancy Lopez, on the driving skills of Davies*

"She doesn't yell 'Fore,' she yells 'Lift off.' You don't watch her ball, you track it. An unidentified flying object entering orbit."

> *Jim Murray*

DRIVERS

"Nobody else is that stupid."

> *Rocky Thompson, on how he knew that he was the only player using a 54-inch driver*

"You don't bail out on your honey, but it was time to win a golf tournament."

> *Lee Trevino, on using a 1-iron instead of his driver on the 18th hole of a tournament*

"Hitch up my girdle and let it rip."

> *Amy Alcott, describing her style at the tee*

"The point is that it doesn't matter if you look like a beast before or after the hit, as long as you look like a beauty at the moment of impact."

> *Seve Ballesteros*

"I can airmail the golf ball, but sometimes I don't put the right address on it."

> *Jim Dent, recognized as one of golf's longest drivers*

"I'll take a two-shot penalty, but I'll be damned if I'm going to play the ball where it lies."

> *Elaine Johnson, after her tee shot hit a tree and caromed into her bra*

"It would have been a hell of a ride."

> *Jack Nicklaus, on seeing an ant on top of the golf ball he was about to hit*

"Through years of experience I have found that air offers less resistance than dirt."

> *Jack Nicklaus, on teeing a golf ball*
> *very high*

"The older you are, the longer you used to be."
> *Chi Chi Rodriguez*

"Art said he wanted to get more distance. I told him to hit it and run backward."

> *Ken Venturi, at a roast for columnist*
> *Art Rosenbaum*

EAGLES

"I've never done that in the heat of battle. Usually, I do it in tournaments where I miss the cut."

> *George Archer, on hitting an eagle 2*
> *on his way to winning a tournament*

"It just happened that the hole got in the way. I was trying to make 4 and I made 3."

> *Fuzzy Zoeller, explaining an eagle 3*

41

"**W**hy don't you ask Mr. Dunlop?"

> *Ben Hogan, after Gary Player, who endorsed Dunlop clubs, asked for advice from Hogan, who had his own line of clubs*

"**I** like the way my wallet feels in them."

> *Johnny Miller, asked if he liked the line of clothes he endorsed*

"**Y**ou've got to look like one to sell those things."

> *Arnold Palmer, on why rotund golfer Bob Murphy had endorsements from a watermelon company*

"**I**t's gotten to the point where you can't tell race car drivers from professional golfers."

> *Lee Trevino, on patch advertisements worn by golfers*

EQUIPMENT

"Give me golf clubs, fresh air, and a beautiful partner and you can keep my golf clubs and the fresh air."
> *Jack Benny*

"It only takes a few seconds to realize that this is more appropriate than keeping the remains in an urn on the mantel, or a shoe box in the closet."
> *Jay Knudsen, entrepreneur, on marketing the idea of putting cremated remains of golfers into shafts of favorite golf clubs*

"Yes, and some you don't want to use."
> *Johnny Miller, asked if he used all his clubs in a tournament*

FAIRWAYS

"I went fishing the other day and I missed the lake with my first cast."
> *Ben Crenshaw, on his trouble with keeping shots on the fairway*

"When I get out on that green carpet called a fairway, manage to poke the ball right down the middle, my surroundings look like a touch of heaven on earth."

Jimmy Demaret

"Fifty percent of the fairways we play on today are better than 90 percent of the greens we played 30 years ago."

Jim Ferree

"It's a tan like mine. It tells you the player is spending a lot of time out on the fairway and the greens—and not in the trees."

Lee Trevino, on the sign of a good golfer

NICK FALDO

"To me, he's very boring. He's never in the trees or in the water. He's not the best driver, not the best putter. He's just the best at everything."

Fred Couples

"That's the trouble with Nick. The only time he opens his mouth is to change feet."

> David Feherty, on the sometimes controversial Faldo

"You look at Faldo and you have to resist the temptation to look at the back for the knobs."

> Jim Murray, on the robotlike play of Faldo

FAMILY AFFAIR

"Now that I have two daughters, I realize if a fellow like me came around and dated my girls, I don't think I would let him in the front door."

> George Archer

"It is a sport in which the whole American family can participate—fathers and mothers, sons and daughters alike. It offers healthy respite from daily toil, refreshment of body and mind."

> Dwight Eisenhower

"He's just perfect for mounting."

> *Mike Hulbert, pro golfer and avid fisherman, on his 8-pound, 3-ounce son*

"Ayako Okamoto, but you're second, Mom."

> *Ashley Knight, five-year-old daughter of Nancy Lopez, on her favorite golfer*

"It's nice to look down the fairway and see your mother on the left and your father on the right. You know that no matter whether you hook it or slice it, somebody is going to be there to kick it back in the fairway."

> *Larry Nelson*

"I don't know. I've never been anyone else's son."

> *Gary Nicklaus, asked if it was difficult being Jack's son*

"I owe a lot to my parents, especially my mother and father."

> *Greg Norman*

"When you see anyone else carrying a baby out here, he's the grandfather."

> *Charles Owens, Senior Tour Player, on having a three-month-old daughter at the age of 56*

"Some people think I'm his daughter, but he's only 11 years older than I am. I wouldn't mind being related, though—especially to his money."

> *Sandra Palmer, golf pro, when asked if she is related to Arnold*

"There are the fans and the people who don't know him at all. Then there are a few people very close to him. I call him Arnie. His friends call him Arnold."

> *Winnie Palmer, Arnold Palmer's wife, on the two groups that call her husband Arnie*

"I asked him once, and he almost broke my arm."

> *Chris Perry, pro golfer, when asked if his uncle, Gaylord Perry, ever threw a spitter*

"Jack Nicklaus is my idol. He's proven he's the greatest golfer in the world."

> *Wayne Player, son of Gary*

"Folks always painted me like something out of 'Li'l Abner'; but I'm proud of where I was born, and proud of the folks I came from."

> *Sam Snead, born in Ashwood, West Virginia*

FASHION SHOW

"Winning is only part of the thing. I wanted people to enjoy seeing me, and I figured if I had fun, they'd have fun."

> *Jimmy Demaret, on his wardrobe*

"If you don't send me a couple hundred pounds a week, I'm going to start wearing your clothes."

> *Simon Hobday, a golfer who was not very fashion-conscious, when asked what he wrote in a letter to the manufacturer of Munsingwear, a line of clothes endorsed by many other European golfers*

48

"I have too much money invested in sweaters."

> *Bob Hope, on why he will never give up golf*

"Emmett Kelly picks out his clothes. . . . Doug looks like he took a bad trip through a paint factory."

> *Don Rickles, on the colorful wardrobe of Doug Sanders*

FIRST ROUND

"Like I always say, the slums of Chicago are full of first-round leaders."

> *Peter Jacobsen, on shooting a 67 in the first round of the Masters*

FOREPLAY

"Golf and sex are about the only things you can enjoy without being good at it."

> *Jimmy Demaret*

"My wife is flying out here tonight. I haven't seen her in two weeks and I'm horny, so that should help."

Ken Green, on his chances of winning the Canadian Open

"Dan would rather play golf than have sex anyday."

Marilyn Quayle

"I can't wait until we make an eagle."

Chi Chi Rodriguez, on his attractive partner in a mixed-pairs tournament giving him a kiss every time they birdied

FORETHOUGHT
(THE MENTAL GAME)

"The best players fail the most because they are in the hunt all the time. You learn to handle it—accept it or you don't survive."

Deane Beman

"The trouble with me is I think too much. I always said you have to be dumb to play good golf."

JoAnne Carner

"I've tried to pay attention and not look around so much. But there's a lot to look at."

Fred Couples, on concentration in golf

"It's a compromise between what your ego wants you to do, what experience tells you to do, and what your nerves let you do."

Bruce Crampton, on concentration in golf

"I'm about five inches from being an outstanding golfer. That's the distance my left ear is from my right."

Ben Crenshaw

"I believe most of us would be restored to golfing health all the more quickly if we could make for ourselves a self-denying ordinance, and refrain from thinking for the minimum of one whole round."

Bernard Darwin, longtime golf writer for the Times *of London*

"I was attracted to this show for the same reason I'm attracted to golf: the high degree of difficulty and endless hope for improvement."

> *Glenn Frey, on his short-lived television show*

"You swing your best when you have the fewest things to think about."

> *Bobby Jones*

"I do not want to think. I want to play golf."

> *Santiago Luna, asked about his chances in the 1991 British Open*

"I never think about anything during the swing. I just hit it. The same thing with batting. Once you're in the box, it's too late."

> *Mickey Mantle, on hitting a golf ball and a baseball*

"Golf is not a creative game. A creative actor will reach the top of his profession. So will a creative basketball player. But a golfer whose mind is creative won't make it."

> *Craig T. Nelson*

"If you have to remind yourself to concentrate during competition—you've got no chance to concentrate."
Bobby Nichols

"I don't play golf to feel bad. I play bad golf and still feel good."
Leslie Nielsen

"You must attain a neurological and biological serenity in chaos. You cannot let yourself be sabotaged by adrenaline."
Mac O'Grady, on the key to playing good golf

"The worst club in my bag is my brain."
Chris Perry

"Thinking instead of acting is the No. 1 golf disease."
Sam Snead

"I have a bad attitude right now. And that's much worse than a bad golf swing."
Payne Stewart, on missing the cut in the 1994 Masters

"The person I fear most in the last two rounds is myself."

> *Tom Watson*

"I'll tell you one thing about chasing the little white ball. Make what you want out of it, but it's all on the greens—and half of that's in your head."

> *Tom Weiskopf*

FRIENDLY WAGERS

"I'd like to be able to bet as much as he does."

> *Laura Davies, on why Michael Jordan is her favorite sports figure*

"I made $215—the $200 I figured I'd lose and the $15 I actually won."

> *Ken Harrelson, on golf hustling*

"I'm not a heavy bettor. I bet for Cokes and stuff. I choke when I play for five dollars."

> *Nancy Lopez*

"Never bet with anyone you meet on the first tee who has a deep suntan, a 1-iron in his bag, and squinty eyes."

Dave Marr

"When I was making 28 bucks a week, the only way I got to go out and play golf was through gambling. It was a great catalyst for me, because I learned to play under pressure. There were times when I was playing that I couldn't afford to lose."

Greg Norman

"Pressure is playing for ten dollars when you don't have a dime in your pocket."

Lee Trevino

"The bookie recognized me. He'd only give me 40 to 1."

Tom Watson, finding out he was 80 to 1 to win the British Open at a betting shop

"Since I don't understand English, I thought they were for me."

> *Isao Aoki, on cheers for Jack Nick-laus, with whom he was paired in the 1980 U.S. Open*

"I wish my name was Tom Kite."

> *Ian Baker-Finch, on signing auto-graphs*

"Golf is one of the easiest sports to get in a player's face. When I'm done, you have to get through the crowd—to get to the locker room. He runs right out of the locker room. I think it's a little simpler."

> *Fred Couples, comparing his experi-ence with crowds to Michael Jordan's*

"It would have been like a friend of mine coming out of the stands to pass the time of day when I was at bat."

> *Joe DiMaggio, asked what he thought of talking to golfers while they were playing*

"Sure I do. After all, I know Tonya Harding."

> *Peter Jacobsen, responding to a fan who said he still had a chance to win even though he was several strokes back*

"You wouldn't yell at somebody playing chess. And, even if you did, it isn't like you would be interrupting him in the middle of a backswing. He can recover. We can't."

> *Peter Jacobsen*

"It's nice to have people watching. They help me find my ball sometimes."

> *Jack Nicklaus II, on large crowds around him*

"The other day we figured up how many autographs I've signed, it's over a million. Think about how many times you sign your name. Think about how long that would take you."

> *Arnold Palmer*

"It hit a spectator, but the ball's OK."

> *Jerry Pate, on a shot that got away*

"Golfers are the only athletes who must dive through hundreds of spectators while in the middle of a game. It's like allowing fans to come out of the football stadium and ask for Joe Namath's autograph between plays."

Dan Sikes

"If I ever find the SOB who came up with these cards, I'm going to shoot him."

Lee Trevino, on the efforts of fans to get Trevino's autograph on his golf sports card

"A little boy came up to me and asked for my autograph. He had a broken arm in a cast. I signed it and asked him what happened. 'Someone catch you teeing it up in the rough?' "

Lee Trevino

"I've got a lot of people rooting for me because there are more poor people than rich people."

Lee Trevino

"I signed Lee Buck Trevino Pit Barbecue, Albuquerque, New Mexico."

> *Lee Trevino, on an attractive woman who asked Trevino to autograph her body*

"I swear Arnold would sign an autograph at a red light. If a guy pulled up to Arnold in a car and asked him for an autograph, Arnold probably would pull over if he could read his lips."

> *Lee Trevino, on Arnold Palmer's reputation as a nice guy*

"Every time you hit a golf shot, there are people who like it and there are people who dislike it. If it goes in the hole, the people who are pulling for you are patting you on the back. And the guy who is pulling for Nicklaus says, 'That lucky SOB—he made a hole in one.'"

> *Lee Trevino*

"Without the people, I'd be playing in front of trees for a couple of hundred dollars."

> *Fuzzy Zoeller*

"A minute? I've got the whole damn weekend."

> *Fuzzy Zoeller, after a fan asked in the second round of a tournament if he had a minute to sign an autograph*

GAMESMANSHIP

"Go up there and miss that 6-footer so I can get to work on this 20-footer."

> *Jimmy Demaret, asked what he would say to psyche out opponents*

"It feels like you can't win."

> *Jim Thorpe, on having a three-shot lead on Jack Nicklaus going to the final hole and Nicklaus saying, "How does it feel to be walking down the last fairway with a three-shot lead over the greatest player to play the game?"*

"Most people don't realize it, but the primary difference between a good game and a bad one lies in the grip."

Julius Boros

"Yes, you're probably right about the left hand, but the fact is that I take my check with the right hand."

Bobby Locke, on criticism of his left-handed grip

"If a lot of people gripped a knife and fork the way they do a golf club, they'd starve to death."

Sam Snead

GOLF AND BASEBALL

"It took me 17 years to get 3,000 hits. I did it in one afternoon on the golf course."

Hank Aaron

"Baseball reveals character; golf exposes it."
Ernie Banks

"Sometimes when I look down at that little white golf ball, I just wish it was moving."
Dusty Baker

"I was three over: one over a house, one over a patio, and one over a swimming pool."
George Brett

"I hit one that far once—I did. And I still bogeyed the hole."
Ron Fairly, on a Mike Schmidt home run

"In baseball you hit your home run over the right-field fence, the left-field fence, the center-field fence. Nobody cares. In golf everything has to go right over second base."
Ken Harrelson

"There's so much to learn and always constant practice in golf. I never worked this hard playing baseball."
Ken Harrelson

"I do. I know how many shots I can give him."

Nancy Lopez, asked who wins when she plays her husband, former major league baseball player Ray Knight

"If I can hit a curveball, why can't I hit a ball that is standing still out on a course?"

Larry Nelson

"Going for a strikeout is like showing off your drive in golf. They pay off on how you putt. I like to save my strikeouts for when I need them."

Gaylord Perry

"I'm the same as any man here who has two arms, two legs, and 4,256 hits."

Pete Rose, sizing up the competition before a match

"I'm doing what every retired Floridian does. Play golf. Watch the sunset. Wait for the mailman. And drive slowly."

Joe Sambito, on retiring from baseball

"Any game where a man 60 can beat a man 30 ain't no game."

> *Burt Shotten, former major league baseball manager, on golf*

"In golf, when we hit a foul ball, we've got to go out and play it."

> *Sam Snead, comparing golf with baseball*

"I tell myself that Jack Nicklaus probably has a lousy curveball."

> *Bob Walk, former major league pitcher, on how he handles golfing frustrations*

"I could only hit balls thrown down at my feet."

> *Tom Watson, on why he didn't pursue a high school baseball career*

"Maybe golfers will want to come here more often."

> *Mark Williamson, Baltimore Oriole's pitcher, on Lee Janzen and Tom Kite both going on to win U.S. Opens after visiting the Oriole clubhouse*

"Man, the worst thing about this is I won't be able to play golf."

> *Charles Barkley, on sustaining a bruised shoulder during the season*

"I hope the Bulls win it so Michael and I can play some golf. Patrick [Ewing] doesn't play golf."

> *Charles Barkley, on why he wanted to play the Bulls instead of the Knicks in the 1993 NBA Finals*

"I needed 'em both."

> *Bob Lanier, on playing in a threesome with a doctor and a priest*

"It's so ridiculous to see a golfer with a one-foot putt and everybody is saying 'Shhh' and not moving a muscle..Then we allow 19-year-old kids to face a game-deciding free throw with 17,000 people yelling."

> *Al McGuire*

"The worst thing about getting fired by the Sixers was having enough time to work on my golf game—and finding out how bad it is."

Doug Moe

"In a team sport, you can go out and make your own breaks. You can make a tackle. You can jump up and block Julius Erving's shot. In golf, you're all alone. Sometimes it's hard. I can't run out and jump on Jack Nicklaus's back."

Andy North

"Only on days ending in *y*."

Jerry West, asked how many days a week he played golf after he retired from basketball

GOLF AND BOWLING

"One of the advantages bowling has over golf is that you seldom lose a bowling ball."

Don Carter

"After losing to Florida the way we did last year, it might not be a good idea for me to get out on a boat with some of our alumni."

> *Bobby Bowden, on going golfing with alumni but refusing to go on fishing trips with them*

"If there were no professional football, you wouldn't find four or five guys to put out there. People pay to play golf. Nobody plays football for nothing, at least not after the age of 21."

> *John Brodie, on why golf is a participant sport and football is a spectator sport*

"My golf game reminds me of Woody Hayes's football game—three yards and a cloud of dust."

> *Bill Dooley, Wake Forest football coach*

"It's time I got my golf game back in shape."

> *Otto Graham, former football great,
> on why he retired as athletic director
> of the U.S. Coast Guard Academy*

"Three out of four are guaranteed to go up the middle."

> *Jeff Hostetler, on Joe Paterno golf
> balls*

"There is one big difference. You're standing still in golf. Stand still in football and you're dead."

> *Hale Irwin, on the difference between
> golf and football*

"My best score ever is 103. But I've only been playing 15 years."

> *Alex Karras*

"I refuse to spend an afternoon in April watching Marino and Elway square off on the 18th tee, locked atop the leaders board at 16 over."

> *Ed Shiffer, writer for* Pro Football
> Weekly, *on the proposed Pro Athletic
> Golf League*

"Don't blame me. Blame the foursome ahead of me."
Lawrence Taylor, on why he was late for a Giants' practice

"I like golf because I can go out and hit a little white ball that doesn't move and doesn't hit back. It should be easy, but it isn't."
Lawrence Taylor

"They ought to be good. They play more golf than we do."
Fuzzy Zoeller, on several NFL quarterbacks getting birdies at a tournament

GOLF AND HOCKEY

"It gets discouraging when you see Wayne Gretzky shoot a puck harder than you can hit a golf ball."
Grant Fuhr

GOLF AND
HORSE RACING

"That's equivalent to a duffer shooting par 72 after one lesson."

Del Miller, on Arnold Palmer driving a pacer a mile in 2 minutes and 9 seconds after only an hour of training

GOLF AND
RACE CAR DRIVING

"Heck no. It's from the six rounds of golf I played in the last five days."

Bobby Rahal, race car driver, when asked if his sore back was caused by an accident in his car

GOLF AND SOCCER

"It was either soccer or golf, and I couldn't kick with those guys."

> *Ken Green, on why he took up golf at age 12 while living with his parents in Honduras*

GOLF AND TENNIS

"I'd love to see John McEnroe join the PGA Tour, just so we could kick him out."
> *Peter Jacobsen*

"Grass? Give me a bucket of balls and a sand wedge. Sure I like grass."

> *Ivan Lendl, on claims he doesn't like playing on grass*

"I have great admiration for Jimmy Connors. In fact, my name used to be Connors, but I changed it for business reasons."

> *Chi Chi Rodriguez, on meeting Jimmy Connors*

"I hate the second serve. If they don't get the first one in, it's a mulligan."

Chi Chi Rodriguez

"Golf is like tennis. The game doesn't really start until the serves get in."

Peter Thomson

GOLF BALLS

"I don't like #4 balls. And I don't like fives, sixes, or sevens on my card."

George Archer, asked if he had any superstitions

"I've been playing with a white ball for 20 years, and I'll keep playing it—unless somebody comes up with the right numbers. For $50,000, I'd paint my driver pink."

Andy Bean, on using colored golf balls

"Titleist has offered me a big contract not to play its balls."

Bob Hope

"My caddie would not let me replace the ball. Obviously, he thought it was a lucky ball. He was right."

> *Hale Irwin, after his ball hit a rock, landed back on the fairway, and he went on to win the tournament*

"A range ball in a new box of Titleists."

> *Gary McCord, self-description*

"A golf ball is like a clock. Always hit it at 6 o'clock and make it go toward 12 o'clock. But make sure you're in the same time zone."

> *Chi Chi Rodriguez*

GOLF BASHERS

"I prefer to take out the dog."

> *Princess Anne, on golf*

"Golf requires less movement at the moment of truth than bowling and attains the same nervous aerobic level as a match of championship pool."

> *Eliot Berry, Tennis magazine writer*

"Golf is not a sport—it's an artistic exercise like ballet. You can be a fat slob and still play golf."
John McEnroe

"If I had my way, any man guilty of golf would be barred from any public office in the United States and the families of the breed would be shipped off to the white slave corrals of Argentina."
H. L. Mencken

"I'm still not sold on the idea of a channel that delivers 24 hours of chubby guys in bad clothes speaking in jargon that only they understand."
Mark Preston, tennis writer, on a 24-hour-golf TV channel

"You can't call it a sport. You don't run, jump, you don't shoot, you don't pass. All you have to do is buy some clothes that don't match."
Steve Sax

"Golf is a good walk spoiled."
Mark Twain

"How can I have intimidated the hitters if I looked like a goddamn golf pro?"

> *Al Hrabosky, former major league re-*
> *lief pitcher who was forced to shave*
> *his menacing beard*

"I don't want 400 members telling me what to do and only talking to me when something goes wrong."

> *Chi Chi Rodriguez, on why he would*
> *never be a golf pro at a country club*

GOLFTOONS

"Guys like me can have a beautiful woman. We make them laugh. Just look at Roger Rabbit."

> *J. C. Anderson, on his beautiful wife*

"The ideal build for a golfer would be strong hands, big forearms, thin neck, big thighs, and a flat chest. He'd look like Popeye."

> *Gary Player*

"One thing about golf is you don't know why you play bad and why you play good."

George Archer

"Golf is an awkward set of bodily contortions designed to produce a graceful result."

Tommy Armour

"A tolerable day, a tolerable green, a tolerable opponent—they supply, or ought to supply, all that any reasonably constituted human should require in the way of entertainment."

Earl of Balfour, former Prime Minister of Great Britain

"It's not how fast you get there, but how long you stay."

Patty Berg, on the true test of a great golfer

"Golf is a game you never can get too good in. You can improve, but you never can get to where you master the game."

Gay Brewer

"Golf is not, on the whole, a game for realists. By its exactitudes of measurements it invites the attention of perfectionists."

Heywood Hale Broun

"Golf is an expensive way of playing marbles."

G. K. Chesterton

"Playing golf is like chasing a quinine pill around a cow pasture."

Winston Churchill

"Golf is a game whose aim is to hit a very small ball into an even smaller hole, with weapons singularly ill designed for that purpose."

Winston Churchill

"Golf is an open exhibition of overweening ambition, courage deflated by stupidity, skill soured by a whiff of arrogance."

Alistair Cooke

"Golf is like love. One day you think you are too old, and the next day you want to do it again."

Roberto De Vicenzo

"Playing the game I have learned the meaning of humility. It has given me an understanding of futility of the human effort."

Abba Eban

"A golf course is nothing but a poolroom moved outdoors."

Barry Fitzgerald, in the movie Going My Way

"Golf is a mystery—as much as one as the universe, solar system, electricity, or ironic affinities."

Paul Gallico

"Golf is the toy department of life. So it should be enjoyable."

Herb Graffis, golf writer

"Make the hard ones look easy and the easy ones look hard."

Walter Hagen

"Golf is golf. You hit the ball, you go find it. Then you hit it again."

Lon Hinkle, pro golfer

"This is a game of misses. The guy who misses the best is going to win."

Ben Hogan

"If you watch a game, it's fun. If you play it, it's recreation. If you work at it, it's golf."

Bob Hope

"There are no pars, birdies, or bogeys—just numbers. Just string them together and add 'em up."

Peter Jacobsen

"One of the most fascinating things about golf is how it reflects the cycle of life. No matter what you shoot—the next day you have to go back to the first tee and begin all over again and make yourself into something."

Peter Jacobsen

"It is nothing new or original to say that golf is played one stroke at a time. But it took me many years to realize it."

Bobby Jones

"I do not advocate unorthodox golf, but I make provisions for it."

Homer Kelley

"It is almost impossible to remember how tragic a place the world is when one is playing golf."

Robert Lynd, English writer

"Serenity is knowing that your worst shot is still going to be pretty good."

Johnny Miller

"Golf is so popular simply because it is the best game in the world in which to be bad."

A. A. Milne

"Golf is not a game, it's bondage. It was obviously devised by a man torn with guilt, eager to atone for his sins."

Jim Murray

"For most players, golf is about as serene as a night in Dracula's castle."

Jim Murray

"Golf without mistakes is like watching haircuts. A dinner without wine."

Jim Murray

"Golf is the cruelest of sports. Like life, it's unfair. It's a harlot. A trollop. It leads you on. It never lives up to its promises. . . . It's a boulevard of broken dreams. It plays with men. And runs off with the butcher."

Jim Murray

"When you play the game for fun, it's fun. When you play it for a living, it's a game of sorrows."

Gary Player

"Golf is a puzzle without an answer. I've played the game for 40 years and I still haven't the slightest idea how to play."

Gary Player

"You are meant to play the ball as it lies, a fact that may help to touch on your own objective approach to life."

Grantland Rice

"Golf is the most fun you can have without taking your clothes off."

Chi Chi Rodriguez

"A passion, an obsession, a romance, a nice acquaintanceship with trees, sand, and water."

Bob Ryan, sportswriter

"Golf is not just an exercise; it's an adventure, a romance . . . a Shakespeare play in which disaster and comedy are intertwined."

Harold Segall

"It's a faithless love, but you hit four good shots and you've started your day right."

Dinah Shore

"I like golf 'cause—well, I reckon I jes' love to play the game."

Sam Snead

"The name of the game is to get the ball in the hole and pick up the check. It's a nice feeling."

Sam Snead

"Sometimes it seems like a man ain't the master of his own destiny. . . . The ball takes a funny little bounce here or a putt takes a funny little turn."

Sam Snead

"You tend to get impatient with poor shots or less-than-perfect shots, but you have to remember less-than-perfect shots win Opens. They are part of the game, and you have to learn to deal with them."

Curtis Strange

"Most golfers prepare for disaster. A good golfer prepares for success."

Bob Toski

"Most people play like Magellan. They're all over the world."

Bob Toski

"Diversification is for big companies, not little companies like myself. I stick with something I know—golf."

Lee Trevino

"I can tell right away if a guy is a winner or a loser just by the way he conducts himself on the course."
Donald Trump

"You can get close enough to mastering the game, to feel it, to breathe it, maybe to smell it. But you can't master it, not for a long time."
Tom Watson

"The uglier a man's legs are, the better he plays golf. It's almost a law."
H. G. Wells

"Golf is a game of days, and I can beat anyone on my day."
Fuzzy Zoeller

GRAND SLAM

"That gives me the Greater Slam."
Mark Brooks, on the Greater Hartford, Greater Greensboro, and Greater Milwaukee being the three victories of his career

GREAT ROUNDS

"I was so far in front, I felt that I was bulletproof."
>   *Raymond Floyd, on winning a tourna-*
>   *ment by five strokes*

"The greatest round a dead man ever shot."
>   *Tom Weiskopf, on shooting a 69 with*
>   *a severe case of flu*

KEN GREEN

"I played a practice round with Hubert [Green] the other day, and when we got to the ninth green, I heard a fan say, 'Why does Hubert have two caddies?'"
>   *Ken Green, on his obscurity on the*
>   *Tour*

WALTER HAGEN

"Walter broke 11 of the Ten Commandments."
>   *Fred Corcoran*

"He exhibited so supreme a confidence that they [his opponents] could not get it out of their minds and could not live against it."
Bernard Darwin

"Hagen's in golf to live—not to make a living."
Chick Evans

"I had a lot of fun playing golf and met a lot of people. I met kings and queens. Golf has always been good to me, and I hope I did a little to help golf."
Walter Hagen

"All the professionals who have a chance to go after the big money today should say a silent thanks to Walter Hagen each time they stretch a check between their fingers. It was Walter who made professional golf what it is."
Gene Sarazen

HAIR IT IS (OR ISN'T)

"When I had hair, they'd just invented dirt."
Miller Barber

"Worst haircut I've ever seen in my life. And I've had a few bad ones. It looks like he has a divot over each ear."

David Feherty, on a John Daly haircut

"I had a lot more hair then—and it was a different color."

Raymond Floyd, on the changes in his 30 years in golf

"I had a two-shot lead. I was only 15 feet from the hole. And I knew the photographers were going to take my picture."

Ralph Guldahl, on pausing to comb his hair on the 18th hole of the 1937 U.S. Open

"Last night when I took a shower, I found a pencil behind my ear and I didn't know how long it had been there."

Bunky Henry, on his long hair

"Every time I look down, I think I'm in the rough."

Jack Lemmon, on growing a mustache

"It reminds me of a good 3-wood lie."

> *Carol Mann, on former football coach*
> *Bum Phillips's crew cut*

"I don't have time to sit under a hair dryer every morning like a girl. If basketball and football players want to grow so much hair, they want to look like apes, that's their business and none of mine."

> *Doug Sanders, on long hair*

HALL OF FAME

"I cannot find a job that pays me $700,000 a year, so until I do, I'll be right here."

> *Pat Bradley, asked if she would retire*
> *after her automatic entrance into the*
> *LPGA Hall of Fame*

"If we don't change [requirements], then pretty soon there's going to be a bunch of old ladies in there, and then pretty soon those old ladies are going to die, and then it's going to be the Dead Hall of Fame."

> *Patty Sheehan, on the difficulty of*
> *qualifying for the LPGA Hall of Fame*

"It was a great honor to be inducted into the Hall of Fame. I didn't know they had a caddie division."

Bob Hope

"My hands were shaking on the last putt. The only problem with that is you never know which shake is going to hit the putt."

Patty Sheehan, on the win that qualified her for the Hall of Fame

HANDICAP

"If you break 100, watch your golf. If you break 80, watch your business."

Joey Adams

"I have an insane desire to shave a stroke or two off my golf handicap."

Alistair Cooke, on why he was retiring from "Masterpiece Theater"

"Nothing goes down slower than a golf handicap."

Bobby Nichols

"The beauty about golf is that the ball doesn't know how big you are."

Claude Harmon, on the importance of size in golf

"He and I have very similar games. Jeff's a smart, strong-minded player who doesn't make many mistakes. The only difference is that I'm a foot and a half taller."

Sandy Lyle, comparing himself to the 5'7" Jeff Sluman

"I've got a lot of power when I get hold of the ball. I'm only 5'8", but I'm broad through the shoulders. I'm the Jewish Yogi Berra."

Don Rickles

"He was the only man around who needed a lifeguard to take a shower."

Sam Snead, on the 5'7", 130 pound Bob Toski

"She is so small, she might get lost in an unreplaced divot."

> *Bob Toski, on Judy Rankin*

"If I got in the ring with a guy six feet tall, I'd bite him on the legs."

> *Ian Woosnam, 5'4½", on how he boxed*

"When you're little and you hit the ball a long way, they love it. There's always some big guys around if you're looking for one. There's not many of us littles."

> *Ian Woosnam, on attracting big crowds*

BEN HOGAN

"Ben Hogan didn't have the prettiest swing in the world, but Ben Hogan knew his game better than anyone else knew theirs."

> *Harvey Penick*

"Nobody covered the flag like Hogan."

> *Gene Sarazen*

"Ben Hogan just knows something about hitting the golf ball the rest of us don't know."
Mike Souchak

"Ben Hogan had three fairways—right, center, and left. The rest of us were lucky we had one. Hogan always hit a shot with the next shot in mind."
Jimmy Thomson

HOLE IN ONE

"Man blames fate for other accidents but feels personally responsible for a hole in one."
Martha Beckman

"All I could think of was, 'Good, I don't have to putt.'"
Mike Blewett, USC golfer, on a hole in one

"I used to play golf with a guy who cheated so badly that he once had a hole in one and wrote down zero on his scorecard."
Bob Bruce

"A spectator said, 'I don't think you understand. You have to hit the hole, not the car.'"

> *Mary Dwyer, pro golfer, after hitting the car that would be awarded to any player in the tournament who shot a hole in one*

"I dreamed I made 17 holes in one, and then on the 18th hole I lipped the cup and I was madder than hell."

> *Ben Hogan*

"It was a hole-in-one contest and I had a three."

> *Abe Lemons, describes how he missed winning a car in a tournament by two strokes*

"In my 57 years of golf, this hole in one is my first ever. To think how many balls I have hit in my life— I was running out of time."

> *Louise Suggs, former LPGA player*

"To me, it's like fishing. If you fish, you'll catch the fish. If you play golf, you'll get holes in one. It seems easy. That's my attitude."

> *David Warren, plumber in North Carolina who has had five holes in one*

"I can explain that shot. Arnold just moved his wallet to the other pocket."

> *Ben Crenshaw, joking about a hook shot Palmer hit during the Skins Game*

"I hate a hook. It nauseates me. I could vomit when I see one. It's like a rattlesnake in your pocket."

> *Ben Hogan*

"You can talk to a fade, but a hook won't listen to you."

> *Lee Trevino*

BOB HOPE

"I've done as much for golf as Truman Capote has done for sumo wrestling."

> *Bob Hope*

"I didn't do anything. I just got well."

> *Frank Beard, on declining his nomination for the Ben Hogan Award for returning to tournament play after a long illness*

"Lee Trevino doesn't want to talk about his back operation. That's all behind him."

> *Don Criqui*

"If I want any sympathy, I have to call up my parents."

> *Beth Daniel, on winning a tournament despite a bad shoulder*

"You know what we should have done? Take Greg skiing."

> *Brad Faxon, on Greg Norman easily winning the Tournament Players Championship after Mark Calcavecchia, Phil Mickelson, and Mark Wiebe were sidelined by skiing injuries*

"Dear Ike, I'm five up on you."

> *Lloyd Mangrum, recuperating from his seventh heart attack while President Eisenhower was recuperating from his second*

"This definitely puts my skydiving plans on hold."

> *Phil Mickelson, on recovering from a broken leg he suffered while skiing*

"Reporters used to ask me questions about the condition of my game. Now all they want to know about is the condition of my health."

> *Jack Nicklaus, on getting older*

INSTRUCTORS

"Don't tempt me, you simpleton."

> *Tommy Armour, to an irate student complaining to Armour about his shooting at squirrels during practice. The student said, "When will you stop that and take care of me?"*

"We've got a society now looking for answers any-where. They might go to a car wash to take a lesson."

Jackie Burke, Jr., on people's search for the perfect swing

"Take two weeks off and then quit the game."

Jimmy Demaret, asked for advice by a struggling golfer

"The practice ground is an evil place. It's full of so-called coaches waiting to pounce. You can see them waiting to dish their mumbo jumbo. To hell with coaches."

Ernie Els

"If you expect a miracle, you should expect to pay for one."

Derek Hardy, Beth Daniel's coach who charged $1,000 for one lesson and 13 lessons for $140

"I used to scrape for a living trying to get people to take lessons. Now everybody wants a lesson. . . . But you know I can't teach any better."

Lee Trevino, on his sudden fame

"I've never had a coach in my life. When I find one who can beat me, then I'll listen."

Lee Trevino

DON JANUARY

"Don January's playing with all the passion and verve of a meter reader."

Vin Scully, on January's slow play

"January shoots low when the money's high."

Lee Trevino, on January's clutch play

JOB FRONT

"My wife said to me the other day, 'My God, you may get to 65 without ever working a day in your life.'"

John Brodie, after a career as a football player, announcer, and a member of golf's Senior Tour

"I'm a vice president in charge of special marketing. That means I play golf and go to cocktail parties. I'm pretty good at my job."

Mickey Mantle

"But I was so unqualified, no one would have me. What else can you do when you've been out here 19 years?"

Leonard Thompson, after applying for other jobs during a 12-year drought between tournament wins

"My conscience hurt me. I hate to play golf when I should be out working, so the only thing to do was quit working."

Jim Umbracht, former major league pitcher who had an off-season job as a salesman for the Houston Colts

BOBBY JONES

"Bobby Jones and Harry Vardon combined exquisiteness of art with utterly relentless precision in a way not given to other golfers."

Bernard Darwin

"I'll be playing center for the Bulls before he's on the Tour."

> *Peter Jacobsen, on Jordan's prospects as a professional golfer*

"Davis Love III turned me on to golf when we were at North Carolina by showing me it wasn't a sissy game."
> *Michael Jordan*

"I think my skills are at that level. Plus Birmingham has some nice golf courses."

> *Michael Jordan, on being sent to the Birmingham Barons, the White Sox Double A minor league team*

"President Clinton has come up with a new plan to cut the deficit and not raise taxes. He's going to play golf with Michael Jordan."

> *Jay Leno, on Jordan's huge gambling debt*

"No, Trevino speaks Mexican."

> *Seve Ballesteros, asked if he and Trevino speak Spanish when they converse*

"I learn English from American pros . . . that's why I speak so bad. I call it PGA English."

> *Roberto de Vicenzo*

"They call it golf because all of the other four-letter words were taken."

> *Raymond Floyd*

"You know, this is like having Billy Martin in your pocket."

> *Mickey Mantle, on using a device on the golf course that utters curses at the push of a button*

"American and English."

> *Peter Teravainen, American pro golfer, when asked the languages he picked up during his six years of playing in Europe and Asia*

"Give me my books, my golf clubs, and leisure, and I would ask for nothing more."

> *Earl of Balfour, former Prime Minister of Great Britain*

"Four wasn't quite enough and six was too much."

> *Gil Morgan, asked why he took a five-week summer break from the Tour*

"It will seat 6 fishermen or 12 lovers."

> *Jack Nicklaus, on his 38-foot boat*

"I hunt and fish, then I play golf, and I play golf so I can hunt and fish."

> *Sam Snead*

"The three things I love best in the world are sex, golf, and hunting. Far as I can see, I ain't about to stop doing any of 'em."

> *Sam Snead*

"Bruce Lietzke is talking seriously about retiring from the PGA Tour, which begs the question—How will anyone know?"

>Steve Hershey, USA Today *columnist*

LIFE WISDOM

"Don't hurry. Don't worry. You're only here on a short visit, so don't forget to stop and smell the flowers."

>*Walter Hagen, describing his philosophy of life*

"I tell you privately, it's not going to get better, it's going to get worse all the time. But don't fret. Remember, we play the ball where it lies."

>*Bobby Jones, describing the rare incurable disease that he was afflicted with in his 40s*

"If I see a guy chasing a girl around the swimming pool, I'm going to root for him, but I'm not going to write about it."

> *Dave Hill, on Frank Beard's tell-all book about golf*

"Are you kidding? The only big word I know is *delicatessen*; and I can't even spell it."

> *Lloyd Mangrum, winner of the 1946 U.S. Open, when asked if he was interested in writing a book*

"The smaller the ball used in the sport, the better the book."

> *George Plimpton, on why books about golf and baseball are better than books about football and basketball*

GENE LITTLER

"Bad? I'll tell you something bad about Gene Littler. He putts too damn good."

> Doug Sanders, asked if he had anything negative to say about Gene Littler

BOBBY LOCKE

"He's the only man in the world whose face is a Parker House roll."

> Jimmy Demaret, on Locke's sagging jowls

"That son of a bitch was able to hole a putt over 60 feet of peanut brittle."

> Lloyd Mangrum

LOSING STREAKS

"I feel like I committed a crime—like I was doing something very bad."

> *Seve Ballesteros, on the media beating him up for his bad play in 1993*

"I played so bad, I got a get-well card from the IRS."

> *Johnny Miller, on a terrible 1977 season*

LOW SCORES

"It seemed like every putt I hit, the hole got in the way."

> *Ronnie Black, on hitting a 63 to win a tournament*

"What in the world am I doing in a golf course where guys shoot 61?"

> *Ben Hogan, on trailing two obscure golfers who shot 61s in the first round of a tournament*

"I sure was glad I ran out of holes. I looked down at my hands and arms to see if it was me when I finished with the score."

> Don January, after shooting a 67 at a recent Senior Tour event

"I kept seeing her ass all day bending over to pick her ball out of the hole."

> Hollis Stacy, on Sally Little shooting a last-round 64 to win the Dinah Shore

"Al Geiberger should have to take a test to prove he's a member of the human race."

> Lee Trevino, after Geiberger shot a record 59 at the Danny Thomas Open

LPGA

"I wish it could have been a 54-hole tournament—the last 54."

> JoAnne Carner, after shooting an opening-round 81 and losing the U.S. Women's Open by only a few strokes

"Imagine having a three-foot putt for $4 million on the final hole of the 1985 J & B Pro-Am after winning the other three tournaments. I think that I'd finally find my choking price."

> *JoAnne Carner, on prize money of $4 million to the LGPA winner of the Dinah Shore, the J & B Scotch Pro-Am, and two other tournaments for two years in a row*

"Yeah, dolls."

> *Babe Didrikson, famous golfer, tennis player, basketball player, skater, etc., when asked if there was anything she didn't play*

"I suppose this is a case of woman's inhumanity to man."

> *Joe Flanagan, fired as director of the Woman's European Tour*

"When we complain about conditions, we're just bitches. But when the men complain, people think, 'Well, it really must be hard.'"

> *Betsy King, on golf's double standards*

"Only my backswing."

> *Charles Meehan, LPGA commissioner,*
> *asked if there was anything embar-*
> *rassing in his background*

"This is not the Ice Capades. You don't fall on a double axel and get up and smile and everything's OK, you know."

> *Dottie Mochrie, on her grim de-*
> *meanor on the Tour*

"I've got to get my gander up. That's a goose, isn't it? They get mad. That's what I need, something to get me going."

> *Patty Sheehan, on being more aggres-*
> *sive on her way to winning the 1983*
> *LPGA Championship*

SANDY LYLE

"I sometimes think Sandy plays in a cloud of unconscious competence."

> *Peter Aliss, commentator for the BBC,*
> *on Lyle's style of play*

"A golfer doesn't know how well he can play until he wins one of the big tournaments under pressure."
Gay Brewer

"I always thought Tom was a good player and a good man. I don't think it took a major to make him one."
Tom Kite, Sr., after his son won his first major, the 1992 U.S. Open

"He'd count the Bangkok Four-Ball if you let him."
Jack Nicklaus, on Gary Player counting many tournaments as majors

"If I play bad the week before a major championship, I have something to blame it on."
Lee Trevino, on why he likes playing in smaller tournaments before a major

"He could shoot 66 wearing tweed pants and no underwear."

Anonymous, on how tough Mangrum was

"Lloyd could get down in two from off the earth."
Tommy Bolt

"I want some bodyguards with their heads up. In my racket, you gotta keep your head down."
Lloyd Mangrum, on death threats

MASTERS

"It's amazing how many friends I had in college who called me up. And they all wanted tickets for the Masters."
Billy Andrade

"I don't care about that. The Green Coat is enough for anybody."

> *Billy Casper, on the money he received for winning the Masters*

"There's one mistake in the drawing. Hogan's in the trees and I'm on the fairway."

> *Billy Casper, on a commemorative drawing of great Masters champions, including Casper, Hogan, Nicklaus, and Palmer*

"Twenty-five million people saw Roberto birdie the 17th hole. I think it would hold up in court."

> *Jimmy Demaret, on Roberto de Vicenzo being placed second to Bob Goalby in the 1968 Masters because his partner wrote a 4 instead of birdie 3 on the 17th hole*

"The course is perfection, and it asks perfection."
> *Nick Faldo*

"If you don't get an invitation, it's like being out of the world a whole week."

> *Doug Ford, on being invited to participate in the Masters*

"I give them all the credit in the world for pulling off the scam they do. No matter how they set up the course, everyone shows up. If any other Tour stop did that, nobody would show up."

Ken Green

"People swarm here. There isn't room to walk. They can't sit down. They get pushed around. They hardly get their cars to park or get them out."

Ben Hogan

"The last year's champion serves as the host. He chooses the menu and picks up the tab. When I discovered the cost of the dinner was more than the prize money, I finished second four times."

Ben Hogan

"You get the feeling that Bobby Jones is standing out there with you."

Lee Janzen, on the mystique of the Masters

"I must admit the name was born of a touch of immodesty."

Bobby Jones, the creator of the Masters

"The course wasn't doing anyone a bit of good—just idle ground, so we thought we could add it to grazing lands available for the war effort."

> *Bobby Jones, on using the Masters grounds to help the country prepare for war*

"You know how they say you're supposed to get that funny feeling when you first drive up the driveway under the tree to the clubhouse? Well, I can tell you, it's true. I got so bad, my car started choking and the windows steamed up."

> *Jerry McGee*

"You don't get any automobiles for a hole in one, you get in the history books. You are playing for the ages here—not a paycheck."

> *Jim Murray*

"If you do, you'll be playing here all alone."

> *Byron Nelson, after Ben Hogan won the 1953 Masters by five strokes and said, "I hope to come back next year and play the same caliber of golf"*

"Augusta National is a young man's golf course, and you really need a young man's nerves to play it."

Jack Nicklaus

"The Christians go to Jerusalem to feel spiritual serenity. Muslims go to Mecca. Rock fans go to rock concerts. And golfers, like the birds of San Juan, Capistrano, migrate to Augusta. This place deserves all the accolades bestowed upon it."

Mac O'Grady

"It's like a black widow. It seduces you, entices you, romances you—and then it stings you, kills you emotionally."

Mac O'Grady

"It would be a unique thing for golf if they let me go out and play defense."

Steve Pate, on the frustration of being in contention for the Masters and finishing the course two hours before the eventual winner

"I always said that if they have a golf course like this in heaven, I want to be the head pro."

Gary Player

"Watching Chip Beck play the last four holes of the Masters, one senses he was trying to win the tournament's coveted Green Vest."

> *Ray Ratto, San Francisco Examiner columnist, on Beck playing cautiously in the last few holes of the 1993 Masters despite being only a few shots behind eventual winner Bernhard Langer*

"So many people have come to me since I made that shot, to tell me they saw it. No golf course could hold that many people."

> *Gene Sarazen, on his famous double eagle on the 15th hole of the 1935 Masters*

"I hope I'll never get too old to want to take part in this event, and I don't think I will ever age that much."

> *Sam Snead, on his love of the Masters*

"It was like a children's birthday party. The presents were there, the cake was on the table, and I made a wish. Only, I forgot to blow out the candles."

> *Ed Sneed, after losing a three-stroke lead to Fuzzy Zoeller in the last round of the Masters*

"More."

*Craig Stadler, asked how he was play-
ing in 1991 compared to his Masters-
winning year of 1982*

"One is for temperament, one is for concentration,
one is for anxiety, and I can't remember what the
fourth one is for."

*Payne Stewart, on playing the 1983
Masters with four acupuncture nee-
dles in his ears*

"I learned that when you blow a major championship,
you feel like hell for a month."

*Curtis Strange, asked what lessons he
learned after losing a two-stroke lead
on the 13th hole of the Masters*

"If you don't get goose bumps when you walk into this
place, you don't have a pulse."

Don Sutton

"A hungry dog hunts best."

*Lee Trevino, on why he will not eat
with fellow players before the Masters*

"Life is like sex and sleep. You only get so many ticks in you, and I'm not going to waste 'em on this track."

Lee Trevino, on his problems with the Masters

"They've done $500 worth of renovations on the greens, but I'll bet in the books it's $700,000. A good husband on a weekend could have done it."

Lee Trevino, on the grounds repair done at the Masters

"There aren't many 50-year-olds beating 20-year-olds. I was born at night, but it wasn't last night."

Lee Trevino, on being in the Masters hunt at the age of 50

"I want the Masters bad! I'm going to Augusta in April and eat crow on the front steps."

Lee Trevino, after several years of criticizing the Masters

"If I knew what was going through Jack Nicklaus's head, I would have won this golf tournament."

Tom Weiskopf, asked if he knew what Jack Nicklaus was thinking on his way to winning the 1986 Masters

"The last time I had this much fun, I was having root canal."

> *Larry Ziegler, after finishing a distant*
> *third to Raymond Floyd at the Masters*

MATCH PLAY

"I loved match play. I would study a guy I was playing, just like Ted Williams studied pitchers. I'd look for a weak spot."

> *Sam Snead*

MEDIA WATCH

"One almost expects one of the players to peer into the monitor and politely request viewers to refrain from munching so loudly on cheese and crackers while the golfers are trying to reach the greens."

> *Pete Alfano, writer for* The New York
> Times

"I haven't yet decided whether I'm going to talk to the press this year or not. After all, look at all the publicity Duane Thomas got by not talking to anybody."

>*Frank Beard, on the controversy surrounding his book in 1972*

"It's a good thing this is on TV; otherwise nobody would believe it."

>*Tommy Bolt. In the early days of televised golf, Bob Rosburg hit two great shots in a row to beat Tommy Bolt.*

"I don't like watching golf on TV. I can't stand whispering."

>*David Brenner*

"Who watches golf on TV? Who calls eight friends over and gets a keg of beer? Landscapers, I guess. They sit around the TV, yelling, 'Will you look at that golf path? Pure pea gravel.'"

>*Jeff Cesario, comedian*

"I don't like watching golf on television—but if I were strapped to a chair, there was only one channel, and golf was the only thing on it, I would pray the commentator would be Gary McCord."

>*Norman Chad, television critic*

"I think they need to look at their own lives before they use that pen. I'm sure a lot of those guys in the media don't have perfect lives."

John Daly

"Lord, I hope this isn't going to be a long interview, or I might lose another stroke."

Lou Graham, being interviewed while Tom Watson took a two-stroke lead on him

"Once last year after I'd won four events, someone asked me, 'What kind of year are you having?' Ever hear of a pitcher with a 20–4 record asked what kind of year he's having?"

Betsy King

"I wish he'd move to Texas and run for the Senate. I'd vote for him just to get him off TV."

Fred Marti, pro golfer, on Howard Cosell

"He's going to have to play a lot better next year or he's going to have to watch a lot of me."

Brent Musburger, responding to John Daly's criticism of him

"How can they have my picture? I ain't never been to New York."

Sam Snead, early in his career, upon seeing a New York paper with his picture in it after winning a tournament out west

"I like the pressroom because you can always get something good to eat and drink."

Rocky Thompson, on why he enjoys talking to the media

"The average golfer would rather play than watch. Those who don't play can't possibly appreciate the subtleties of the game. Trying to get their attention with golf is like selling Shakespeare in the neighborhood saloon."

Bob Toski, on why golf and television don't mix

"They don't put announcers in history books."

Claudia Trevino, on why her husband left NBC to play in the Senior Tour

"Almost to a man America's indigenous golf commentators sound like half-wit hillbillies reliving all their yesterdays round a campfire."
>
> *Ian Wooldridge, British writer*

MEDIOCRITY

"My mom hates to start searching for my name from the bottom of the list each week."
>
> *Andrew Magee*

"Mediocre players are just out there messing up the sand traps."
>
> *Lloyd Mangrum*

"There are 23 million golfers in this country and most of them are bad. I'm just one of them."
>
> *Gary McCord*

"The difference is Uecker only played baseball for about five years. I've been dismal at golf for 17 or 18."
>
> *Gary McCord, comparing himself to Bob Uecker*

"My career started slowly and then tapered off."
Gary McCord

"I never knew what top golf was like until I turned professional. Then it was too late."
Steve Melnyk

PHIL MICKELSON

"His future is ahead of him."
Steve Melnyk

CARY MIDDLECOFF

"The way he filled those 72 cavities during the last four days makes me think maybe I was wrong."

> *Bobby Jones, after Middlecoff won the 1955 Masters by seven strokes, on his own efforts, at the urging of Middle-coff's father, to convince Cary to give up golf and go back into dentistry*

"I pulled 7,000 teeth before I found out the army had another dentist."

> *Cary Middlecoff, on his role as a dentist in World War II*

MILITARY WATCH

"You have to let a little air into the war room now and then."

> *Dwight Eisenhower, on enjoyment of golf*

"Orville was on the Tour a year before he stopped saluting his caddie."

> *Bob Hope, on Orville Moody, an ex-marine turned golf pro*

"I started out as a private, but after beating the colonels a few times, I rose to sergeant."

> *Lee Trevino, on playing golf in the marines*

"I didn't say he was the biggest moron in the booth. I said he was the biggest Mormon. Somebody dropped the *m*."

> *Paul Azinger, on the announcing of Johnny Miller*

"I know this sounds cruel, but his win doesn't say a lot for our PGA Tour players."

> *Fred Couples, after Johnny Miller won the 1994 AT&T Pebble Beach Tournament*

MONEY TOUR

"It's just like going to the office. I've done my job, and by doing it, I can provide for my family and prove to my peers that I belong."

> *Frank Beard*

"I was the leading money spender."

> *John Brodie, on his earnings on the PGA Tour*

"If you want it, get it and spend it. It's only money, not something to worship. If you run out, go out and get some more."

Mark Calcavecchia

"How could anyone working eight-to-five generate sympathy for anybody who could win $50,000 in a week?"

Hubert Green

"I never wanted to be a millionaire. I just wanted to live like one."

Walter Hagen

"That's when two of my kids finish college."

Don January, on why June would be his best financial month

"Every kid learning to play golf dreams about winning the Masters, about winning the Open, not about being the leading money winner."

Tom Kite

"I'm third in earnings. And first in spending."

Tony Lema

"No, I never had enough in my pocket for that."

Orville Moody, asked if he would be forced to quit a tournament because of allergies

"Only in America can you explain a man working three days and making $52,500."

Chi Chi Rodriguez

"Money's no good if you use it just as a weapon. . . . If you share it, you'll always have enough. And if you don't, you'll never have enough."

Chi Chi Rodriguez

"I was so poor, I grew up under a sign that said, 'Made in Taiwan.' "

Chi Chi Rodriguez

"The problem is, I'm already over $2 million in spending."

Chi Chi Rodriguez, on having reached a million dollars in career earnings

"I'm working as hard as I can to get my life and my cash to run out at the same time. If I can just die after lunch Tuesday, everything will be perfect."

Doug Sanders

"I never saw a Brinks truck following a funeral procession."

Lee Trevino, on why he spends so much money

"We had so little to eat that when Mom would throw a bone to the dog, he'd have to call for a fair catch."

Lee Trevino

"When I turn 40, I'm going to have to count my money. I'm going to have it stacked around the house in bales, not just bundles."

Lee Trevino, at age 32

"The most dangerous thing I do is drive to the bank. I've got a bad swing and a bad grip, but my banker loves me."

Lee Trevino, on his unorthodox style

"There are no rich Mexicans. They get some money, they call themselves Spanish."

Lee Trevino

ORVILLE MOODY

"I never played with the Lone Ranger before."
> *Chi Chi Rodriguez, on being paired*
> *with Orville Moody, who was wearing*
> *a surgical mask to protect himself*
> *from allergies*

MULLIGANS

"We took a mulligan."
> *Cheryl Kratzert, wife of pro golfer Bill*
> *Kratzert, on being married, divorced,*
> *and then remarried*

"There are no mulligans in that sport."
> *Gary Player, on bungee jumping*

"You can't just say 'Hey, Bob, you're away' or 'Bob, you're going to be matched with Bob Jones here.'"

> *Bob Jones, on a tournament in Detroit featuring only players with the name Bobby Jones*

"Tiger Woods? I thought that was a golf course."

> *Sandy Lyle, asked his opinion of the junior star Tiger Woods*

"I just want to be a household word in my own household."

> *Howard Twitty, on not wanting great fame as a golfer*

NASSAUS

"A man's true colors will surface quicker in a five-dollar Nassau than in any other form of peacetime diversion that I can name."

> *Grantland Rice*

"We couldn't find Michael Jordan, so we could only play for $25."

> Lee Trevino, on playing for $25 Nassaus

BYRON NELSON

"At my best I never came close to the golf Nelson shoots."

> Bobby Jones

JACK NICKLAUS

"I would guess Nicklaus was in one for about 25 years."

> Raymond Floyd, asked if Sandy Lyle's string of victories was the hottest streak he'd ever seen

"If there is anything to this astrology business, Jack Nicklaus must have been born under every sign."

> Gibby Gilbert

"All my life I wanted to play golf like Jack Nicklaus, and now I do."

Paul Harvey, after Nicklaus shot an 83 in a tournament

"He's the only golfer I've ever seen who should be required to play with a handicap."
Bobby Jones

"Palmer and Player played superbly. But Nicklaus played a game with which I'm not familiar."

Bobby Jones, after Nicklaus won the 1965 Masters

"When Jack Nicklaus plays well, he wins. When he plays badly, he finishes second. When he plays terribly, he finishes third."
Johnny Miller

"The rest of us have to be playing well to win, but Jack's so good, he can play mediocre and win."
Johnny Miller

"Around a clubhouse they'll tell you even God has to practice his putting. In fact, even Nicklaus does."
Jim Murray

"The measure of Jack Nicklaus is when he wins, not what he wins. It's how, not how many. Anybody can beat a palm tree and two sand trap courses."
Jim Murray

"It's hard not to play up to Jack Nicklaus's standards when you are Jack Nicklaus."
Jack Nicklaus

"Those steely blue eyes cut right through you."
Jerry Pate, on the competitiveness of Nicklaus

"One day I played nine holes with Jack Nicklaus and I beat him on two of the holes. I knew I was a good player, but that's when I knew I was a great player."
Chi Chi Rodriguez

"He's the only golfer in history who has become a living legend in his spare time."
Chi Chi Rodriguez, on the many extracurricular activities of Nicklaus

"Fine, but the Big Bear is back there staring over my shoulder. You can never forget about him."

Chi Chi Rodriguez, after having a great round and finding himself atop the leader board

"How about that. A blind man's been beating me every day. I wondered why he's always asking me at midnight if I want to go out and play."

Lee Trevino, on Nicklaus complaining about losing sight of a long drive

"For my money, I'd want Jack to play for me if it was one hole or a hundred and one."

Lee Trevino

GREG NORMAN

"I think he wants to be included in the glory of it all, but deep down I don't think he's totally comfortable having the last shot."

Johnny Miller

"Norman makes the rest of us look like we're hitting tennis balls."

Lee Trevino

OH, GOD

"I just hope I don't have to explain all the times I've used His name in vain when I get up there."

Bob Hope, on the frustrations of golf

"I played golf with a priest the other day. . . . He shot par-par-par-par-par. Finally, I said to him, 'Father, if you're playing golf like this you haven't been saving many souls lately.' "

Sam Snead

"That was not golf; it was a visitation from the Lord."

Bill Stout, on Donald Moe playing phenomenal golf, including a birdie on the last hole, to win the Walker Cup

"There are two things you can do with your head down—play golf and pray."

Lee Trevino

"Hold up a 1-iron and walk. Even God can't hit a 1-iron."

> *Lee Trevino, on how to avoid being hit by lightning*

PAIRINGS

"Woosy and I are talking about marriage. He says it's the longest relationship he's ever had."

> *John Daly, on playing all four rounds of the Masters with Ian Woosnam*

"Best blind date I've ever had."

> *Mike Donald, on being paired at the last minute with Vicki Alvarez and winning a mixed-pairs championship in 1984*

"He is so great; you want to prove to him that you can play, too. It is very tough. Some of the younger players, when they get paired with him, can't even draw the club back."

> *Johnny Miller, on being paired with Jack Nicklaus*

"Tony, you don't have to talk. You just have to listen."
Lee Trevino, responding to his partner, Tony Jacklin, who said, "We don't need any conversation today"

ARNOLD PALMER

"I should tithe 25 cents of every dollar I make to Arnie."
Frank Beard

"I never figured out what women saw in him, but I'd like a case of it."
Peter Dobereiner, golf writer

"When you hear someone shout 'You da man,' if he ain't shouting at Arnold Palmer, then it ain't da man."
Ron Green, Charlotte Observer *columnist*

"He has won almost as much money playing golf as I've spent on lessons."
Bob Hope

"Arnold Palmer is the biggest crowd pleaser since the invention of the portable sanitary facility."
Bob Hope

"He's the biggest thing in the desert since sand."
Bob Hope, on Palmer winning the Hope Classic five times

"If I ever needed an eight-foot putt and everything I owned depended on it, I would want Arnold Palmer to putt it for me."
Bobby Jones

"Palmer plays golf like others play football."
Johnny Miller

"He was Dempsey with his man on the ropes, Ruth with a fastball, Montana with a man open."
Jim Murray

"I've always had Arnold's gallery to fight, but I never had to fight Arnold. I've never forgotten that."
Jack Nicklaus

"Anybody who resents Arnold getting more attention than the rest of us doesn't deserve to use his head for more than a hat rack."

Doug Sanders

"If Arnie asked me to shine his shoes, I'd take off my shirt and shine them."

Ken Still, pro golfer and self-proclaimed worshiper of Palmer

"Arnold has more people watching him park the car than we do out on the course."

Lee Trevino

"The fans would like to see Palmer win, but they don't really care. They just want to see him. There never has been a guy who has done as much for sports as Arnie has for golf."

Tom Watson

"Just about the greatest thing a man can do who doesn't play golf for a living. That includes getting kissed by a cheerleader, having cash money in your pocket, owning a faithful dog, and anything that has to do with marriage."

Lewis Grizzard, on shooting his first-ever par game

"Anything I want it to be. For instance, the hole right here is a par 47, and yesterday I birdied the sucker."

Willie Nelson, on what was par on a course he bought in Texas

"I don't fear death, but I sure don't like those three-footers for par."

Chi Chi Rodriguez

"Forget your opponents; always play against par."

Sam Snead

"There are two things not long for this world—dogs that chase cars and pro golfers who chip for pars."

Lee Trevino

PAR-TEE LINES
(POLITICS AND GOLF)

"Whoa, Mama, stay up."
> *Bill Clinton, driving a golf ball at*
> *Martha's Vineyard*

"A lot more people beat me now."
> *Dwight Eisenhower, on how his golf*
> *game deteriorated after his presidency*

"I remember he was so wild that when the word got out that he was taking a lesson, the parking lot was emptied of Cadillacs in five minutes."
> *Max Elbin, pro at the country club*
> *where President Nixon took lessons*

"The pat on the back, the arm around the shoulder, the praise for what was done right, and the sympathetic nod for what wasn't are as much a part of life as golf itself."
> *Gerald Ford*

"Because there's no golf club called a potato wedge."

> *Larry Harrington, Democratic consultant, on why Dan Quayle misspelled the word* potato

"He's the best driver since Ben Hur."

> *Bob Hope, acknowledging that for all the jokes, President Ford was a good golfer*

"Whenever I play with him, I usually try to make it a foursome—the President, myself, a paramedic, and a faith healer."

> *Bob Hope, on Gerald Ford*

"We have 51 golf courses in Palm Springs. He never decides which course he will play until after his first tee shot."

> *Bob Hope, on Gerald Ford*

"It is true that my predecessor did not object as I do to pictures of one's golfing skills in action. But neither, on the other hand, did he ever bean a Secret Service agent."

> *John Kennedy, on why he didn't want pictures taken of him playing golf, unlike President Eisenhower*

"I tried my level best to make Calvin Coolidge president."

> *Ring Lardner, on almost hitting President Harding at a golf tournament. Calvin Coolidge was Harding's vice president*

"I'm awful sorry, honey, but I'd have had 30 more yards if you had gotten out of the way."

> *Tip O'Neill, after hitting a woman on the backside during a tournament*

"If I swing the gavel the way I swing a golf club, no wonder the nation's in a mess."

> *Tip O'Neill*

"In golf, you keep your head down and follow through. In the vice presidency, you keep your head up and follow through. It's a big difference."

> *Dan Quayle*

"He'd rather face Congress than a three-foot putt."

> *Ken Raynor, club pro at the Kennebunkport course where George Bush played*

"Rail splitting produced an unparalleled president in Abraham Lincoln, but golf hasn't produced even a good A-1 congressman."

> *Will Rogers*

"Photographs of me on horseback, yes, tennis, no. And golf is fatal."

> *Teddy Roosevelt, in a letter to William Howard Taft warning Taft never to be seen playing golf*

"I thought I was safe on the fairway."

> *Doug Sanders, after being hit by a shot from Spiro Agnew while walking along the fairway*

"If it was a paying job, someone might run and I might be out."

> *Rocky Thompson, Senior Tour player and mayor of Toco, Texas*

"First, hitting the ball. Second, finding out where it went."

> *Tom Watson, asked what he would focus on in helping President Ford's golf game*

"Politics, like music and golf, is best learned at an early age."

Lawrence Welk

COREY PAVIN

"He plays the game of golf as if he has a plane to catch. As if he were double-parked and left the meter running. Guys move slower leaving hotel fires."

Jim Murray, on Corey Pavin

PGA

"Whatever you do, please don't ever say 'Holy Toledo' to Norman."

Thomas Boswell, after Greg Norman lost the 1986 PGA by a stroke at Inverness in Toledo

"All four days I didn't think. I just hit. Squeaky [his caddie] said kill and I killed it."

John Daly, on coming from nowhere to win the 1991 PGA

"It's so long that figuring distances on some holes, you have to reckon in the curvature of the earth."

> *David Feherty, on the Crooked Stick Golf Club, site of the 1992 PGA*

"The moment you turn your back, the government has created another agency."

> *Lord Halifax, after Gene Sarazen, whom he had never heard of before, met him and told him he was going to the PGA*

"Where can you go to have a good cry?"

> *Mike Reid, on giving away a three-stroke lead on the last three holes to lose the 1989 PGA Championship*

"The most wonderful sound of all is on the first tee at the tournaments when they introduce me as the PGA champion."

> *Dave Stockton, winner of the 1970 PGA*

"If I would have jumped like that in high school, I would have played basketball."

> *Bob Tway, on jumping for joy after winning the PGA title*

PLANES, TRAINS, AND AUTOMOBILES

"They don't have McDonald's up there."

> *John Daly, on why he doesn't like flying*

"At least one of us had a good year."

> *Ray Fisher of Chrysler Corporation, awarding a trophy to Nancy Lopez for being 1979's Player of the Year*

"You don't know what he charged me for the ride out. I'll have to win the damn thing to get back home."

> *Raymond Floyd, on flying to Australia in Greg Norman's private jet to play in Norman's tournament*

"Now I know why they tell you to put your head between your knees on crash landings. You think you're going to kiss your ass good-bye."

> *Terry Hanson, after learning a jet he was in was out of control*

"It doesn't fit through the Wendy's drive-through."

> *Scott Hoch, on selling a Mercedes-Benz he won at a tournament*

"When people ask me my address, I tell them 747 Boeing."

> *Robert Trent Jones, on traveling around the world designing new golf courses*

"I fell in love at first flight."

> *Tony Lema, on marrying an airline attendant*

"I hope to win more of these and start my own dealership."

> *Sally Little, on capturing a tournament for the second year in a row that awarded a Mazda to the winner*

"It was like falling in a giant lift when the cable snapped; only, your stomach stayed on the tenth floor."

> *Ron Meager, golf reporter, on the turbulent 1959 flight of the British Ryder Cup team*

"I must have sat on my bottom for about three years."

Gary Player, on his estimate of having flown over 6½ million miles in his career

GARY PLAYER

"He has milked more success out of his natural ability than any other athlete I know."

Sam Snead

PLAYOFFS

"I do not think you should have a sudden-death playoff to decide a national championship. . . . It's a little too much merely to accommodate television."

Jack Nicklaus, on losing the Canadian Open in a playoff

PRACTICE

"If I practiced putting as much as I practiced swimming, I'd be dangerous."

> *George Archer, on swimming several*
> *hours every day to heal a bad back*

"The more I practice, the luckier I get."
> *Jerry Barber*

"Sometimes I wonder about practice. I've hit about 70,000 golf balls in the last four years, and some days I still play like an amateur."
> *Hubert Green*

"I figure practice puts your brains in your muscles."
> *Sam Snead*

"I used to think pressure was standing over a four-foot putt knowing I had to make it. I learned that real pressure was 65 people waiting for their food with only 30 minutes left on their lunch break."

Amy Alcott, on a part-time job she had as a waitress early in her career

"He may be in bed, but he ain't sleeping."

Walter Hagen, asked if his partying all night the evening before a playoff might be an advantage for his opponent

"I'm shooting the best golf of my life because there's no pressure. The mind destroys you."

Ken Harrelson, on giving up professional golf

"I don't throw up."

Sandra Haynie, on the major difference in her game over the last 20 years

"He doesn't drink. To face that kind of pressure, week after week, you have to drink."

> *Ralph Kiner, on the great early career*
> *of Johnny Miller*

"My butterflies are still going strong. I just hope they are flying in formation."

> *Larry Mize, on playing with a big lead*

"Golf is something you play every week. You can take the pressure off just by telling yourself, 'Well, there's always next week.' You can't do that in the World Series or the Olympics."

> *Calvin Peete*

"The pressure gets worse the older you get. The hole starts to look the size of a Bayer aspirin."

> *Gary Player*

"How do you be funny when you have a six-foot putt for $54,000?"

> *Jack Renner, professional golfer*

"You only tighten up in the last rounds when you are broke."

> *Charlie Sifford*

"Anytime you play golf for whatever you've got, that's pressure. I'd like to see H. L. Hunt go out there and play for $3 billion."

Lee Trevino

"I never heard of them before. I thought it was some kind of sunglasses."

Lanny Wadkins, on rumors of use of beta blockers by top golfers to calm their nerves

"I think it's true that we create our own pressure. If you think about water to the right and a trap to the left and all the things that can go wrong, then you're creating your own pressure."

Tom Weiskopf

"I ain't got no nerves. Once you walk a six-inch beam 30 floors above the ground, a three-foot putt doesn't scare you none."

Walter Zembriski, Senior Tour golfer and former construction worker

"It's like swinging at a golf ball and quitting on the shot . . . like there's no follow-through."

> *Sharron Moran, female golfer, on the difficulties of dating when you are only in town for a week*

"Maybe I'm a miser, but all I need is a toilet, bed, and TV."

> *Brett Ogle, on seeking out cheap places to stay while on the road*

"It is an addicting passion for those who succeed. But for those who fail, a certain demise, decay, and death of their dreams becomes an exercise in bereavement."
> *Mac O'Grady*

"They're playing for so much money, they don't have time to smile."

> *Sam Snead, on players playing like robots on the Tour*

"We are all a bunch of hard bastards. Some of us are just better at not showing it."

>Lee Trevino, on the top players on the Tour

"I'm like a duck. I get up in a new world every day."

>Lee Trevino

"My wife tells me she doesn't care what I do when I'm away, as long as I'm not enjoying it."

>Lee Trevino

PUBLIC COURSES

"Is it public? You can get starting times in seven different languages."

>Tip O'Neill, asked if the golf course named after him was public

"I miss the putt. I miss the putt. I miss the putt. I make."

> *Seve Ballesteros, explaining his four-putt on the 16th green at the 1986 Masters*

"Ninety percent of the putts that fall short don't go in."

> *Yogi Berra*

"Yeah, after each of my downhill putts."

> *Homero Blancas, after shooting a 77 in the first round of the U.S. Open and being asked if he had any uphill putts*

"I enjoy the oohs and aahs from the gallery when I hit my drives. But I'm getting pretty tired of the awws and uhhs when I miss the putt."

> *John Daly*

"That's fine, but I hit my putts as long as my drives."
Laura Davies, on being the longest hitter on the Tour

"All I can do is start it. The Lord handles it from there."
Jimmy Demaret, on putting

"If you're going to miss 'em, miss 'em quick."
George Duncan, on putts

"Short putts are missed because it is not physically possible to make the little ball travel over uncertain ground for three or four feet with any degree of regularity."
Walter Hagen

"If you three-putt the first green, they'll never remember it. But if you three-putt the 18th, they'll never forget it."
Walter Hagen

"Did you ever consider hitting it closer to the hole?"
Ben Hogan, after someone asked him how to be a better putter

"That putt was so good, I could feel the baby applaud."

Donna Horton-White, on making a 25-foot putt while seven months pregnant

"Find a man with both feet firmly on the ground and you've found a man about to make a difficult putt."

Fletcher Knebel, writer

"I've been playing until dark and even then I'm thinking about putting my car on the green so I can putt."

Ivan Lendl

"You drive for show, but putt for dough."

Bobby Locke

"I never believed that a Kite need have that sort of range."

Gary McCord, on Tom Kite sinking an 80-foot putt in the Phoenix Open

"Putting affects the nerves more than anything. I would actually get nauseated over three-footers, and there were tournaments when I couldn't keep a meal down for four days."

Byron Nelson

"When I putt, my emotions collide like tectonic plates. It's left my memory circuits full of scars that won't heal."

Mac O'Grady

"Putting is like wisdom—partly a natural gift and partly the accumulation of experience."

Arnold Palmer

"The man who can putt is a match for anyone."

Willie Park, Jr.

"I never pray to God to make a putt. I pray to God to help me react good if I miss a putt."

Chi Chi Rodriguez

"I played like Doug Sanders and putted like Colonel Sanders."

Chi Chi Rodriguez

"A sick appendix is not as difficult to deal with as a five-foot putt."

Gene Sarazen

"It's so bad I could putt off a tabletop and still leave the ball halfway down the leg."

J. C. Snead, on his putting

"Well, Bob, when you come in off the course, they don't ask you how. They ask you how many."

Sam Snead, after Bobby Jones criticized his sidesaddle putting style

"The ball's got to stop somewhere. It might as well be at the bottom of the hole."

Lee Trevino, stating his putting philosophy

"Arnold Palmer is Mr. Golf; he's fried chicken and apple pie. And him putting with his hands separated is un-American."

Lee Trevino, on Palmer putting with a split-handed grip

"There are many ways of performing the operation successfully. I can claim, however, to be in a position to explain how not to putt. I think I know as well as anybody how not to do that."

Harry Vardon

"The least thing upset him on the links. He missed short putts because of the uproar of butterflies in the adjoining meadows."

P. G. Wodehouse

PUTTERS

"That's a bagful of indecision."

Jackie Burke, on Arnold Palmer bringing eight putters to the Colonial at Fort Worth

"I'd chip it with a 5-iron before I'd use one of those things."

Ben Crenshaw, on extra-long putters

"When it's going good, you love your putter. When it's going bad, it's like it has betrayed you and you want to throw the sucker into a lake."

Ken Green

"I see older guys struggling big time, but they're too worried about their pride. I'm not traditional. I worry about feeding my family."

Brett Ogle, on long putters

"It's a marriage. If I had to choose between my wife and my putter—I'd miss her."

Gary Player

"If I'm going to miss a putt, I want to look good doing it."

Chi Chi Rodriguez, on why he is reluctant to use a long-handled putter

"You got to see that putter to believe it. It's four days older than dirt. It squeaks when I use it."

Chi Chi Rodriguez, on a 60-year-old putter he used in a tournament

"Rex has been a rabbit so long that his nose twitches when he gets around a salad bar."

> *Anonymous, on Rex Caldwell, a long-time rabbit who had a string of good tournaments*

"Because they're always nibbling at the lettuce."

> *Tony Lema, explaining why tournament qualifiers are called rabbits*

"I feel like I've been sprung from jail."

> *Gary McCord, on being a full-fledged member of the Tour and no longer a rabbit*

"I asked why they didn't call some rookie bench-sitter with the Dallas Cowboys, some 270-pound tackle, a toad or a gopher. The reason they don't was because the big football team would stuff their typewriters where the sun don't shine."

> *Jerry McGee, on hating the word* rabbits *for tournament qualifiers*

"I'm so happy to be on the Tour, a little speck in the history of American sports."

> Mac O'Grady, on qualifying for the
> Pro Tour after years of missing it

"Grab him quick. I don't think he signed his card."

> J. C. Snead, on a rabbit that jumped
> on the green and then disappeared

MIKE REID

"Usually, you do not ask Mike Reid how many fairways he missed. You ask him how many water sprinkler lines he missed."

> Gordon White, New York Times columnist, on Reid's straight tee shots

"Baseball players quit playing and they take up golf. Basketball players quit, take up golf. Football players quit, take up golf. What are we supposed to take up when we quit?"

George Archer

"Most people retire to play golf and fish. I do that now."

Julius Boros, on not retiring at age 55

"I play the game because my sole ambition is to do well enough to give it up."

David Feherty

"Don't ever get old."

Ben Hogan, advising a young player upon his own retirement

"When a man retires, his wife gets twice the husband but only half the income."

Chi Chi Rodriguez

"Getting my first Social Security check."

> *Gene Sarazen, at age 72, on his greatest thrill*

"They have other things to go to. I hunt and fish, then I play golf."

> *Sam Snead, on why he was still playing while contemporaries like Hogan, Demaret, and Nelson were retired*

"When I retire, I'm going to get a pair of gray slacks, a white shirt, a striped tie, a blue blazer, a case of dandruff, and go stand on the first tee so I can be a USGA official."

> *Lee Trevino*

TED RHODES

"Ted Rhodes was the best golfer I ever saw, and that includes Arnold Palmer and Jack Nicklaus. If they ever let him play on the PGA Tour, he would have won everything."

> *Charlie Sifford, on Rhodes being discriminated against because he was black*

"I do it not to relax. I do it to make people laugh."
>   *Chi Chi Rodriguez, on his sword-and-hat routine*

"Call me a clown, call me a nice guy, call me serious. Just don't call me collect."
>   *Chi Chi Rodriguez*

"I think I'm going to change my name from Juan to Nine-Juan-Juan. I'm like the rescue squad. Whenever someone needs help, they call for me."
>   *Chi Chi Rodriguez, on his real name of Juan and his role as one of golf's good guys*

"When you're having trouble and topping the ball, it means the ground is moving on you."
>   *Chi Chi Rodriguez*

"I'm playing like Tarzan and scoring like Jane."
>   *Chi Chi Rodriguez*

"I expect to make at least seven mistakes a round. Therefore, when I make a bad shot, I don't worry about it. It's just one of those seven."

Walter Hagen

"Would you rather be broke or have money in the bank?"

Ben Hogan, asked if he would rather be in the lead or a shot or two behind going into the last round

"One minute you're bleeding. The next minute you're hemorrhaging. The next minute you're painting the Mona Lisa."

Mac O'Grady, on a typical round of golf

"I guess it's kind of like the fisherman who caught a 30 pounder and let it get away."

Ken Still, on shooting a 31 on the first nine holes of a round and then shooting a 37 on the back nine

"I don't know the traffic regulations of every city I get to either, but I manage to drive through without being arrested."

> *Lloyd Mangrum, on being assessed many violations as a result of not knowing the rule book*

"I think most of the rules of golf stink. They were written by guys who can't even break a hundred."
> *Chi Chi Rodriguez*

RUNNER-UP

"I'll be in a familiar role next year. I'll be the defending runner-up."

> *Bruce Crampton, on finishing second to Nicklaus in the 1975 PGA and being second in several other majors*

"He has come in second more times than the Washington Generals."
> *Rick Reilly, on Tom Kite*

"We thumped them Iraqis, and now we've beaten the Europeans."

> *Paul Azinger, on the U.S. winning the 1991 Ryder Cup*

"The Ryder Cup team of Americans was comprised of 11 nice guys and Paul Azinger."

> *Seve Ballesteros, on the 1991 American team*

"It's like the America's Cup. I never even heard of it until we lost it."

> *Raymond Floyd, on the Ryder Cup*

"When the Americans apply themselves to winning something as seriously as they have with the Ryder Cup, you have to cope with a very, very ruthless animal."

> *Bernard Gallacher, captain of the 1993 Ryder Cup European team*

"There's no way of getting used to it. For every eight major championships, you get one Ryder Cup."

Tom Kite, on the pressure of Playing for the Ryder Cup

"The No. 1 source of pressure and choking is that you don't want to let your teammates down. It's the only time of the year when you care more about others than yourself."

Johnny Miller

"C'mon, guys, it's not like coming down the stretch at a major. Good gracious, if you make a mistake, you still have 11 other guys helping you."

Jack Nicklaus

"It doesn't matter how many Open championships or titles you may have won. When you stand on the tee at a Ryder Cup match and play for your country, your stomach rumbles like a kid turning up for his first tournament."

Arnold Palmer

"I wouldn't know him if he came up and bit me."

Payne Stewart, on his Ryder Cup opponent Joakim Haeggman

"We're not interested in ancient history. We're going to make history."

> Dave Stockton, captain of Ryder Cup Team, on not choosing Jack Nicklaus for the team

SAND TRAPS

"I stayed in the bunker until I made one. They had to bring me cocktails and dinner."

> JoAnne Carner, on how she got a good sand game

GENE SARAZEN

"When he is in the right mood, he is probably the greatest scorer in the game . . . possibly, that the game has ever seen."

> Bobby Jones

"When Gene takes the field against any golfer, or any array of golfers, the only question in his mind is in the first instance, how many holes it will take to beat his man, and in the second, by what margin is he going to finish in front."

> *O. B. Keeler*

SENIOR TOUR

"If I don't get shot by a jealous husband, I may be around awhile."

> *Jerry Barber, a 74-year-old Senior Tour pro whose mother and father lived to the ages of 103 and 86, respectively*

"I'm going to retire at 40, practice for ten years, then join the Senior Tour when I turn 50."

> *Albert Belle, asked what he was planning to do with his life after baseball*

"You know you're on the Senior Tour when your back goes out more than you do."

> *Bob Bruce*

"What's nice about our tour is you can't remember your bad shots."

> Bob Bruce

"A senior tour? Hell I spent all my life trying to get away from these guys."

> Jackie Burke, Jr., on the early days of the Senior Tour

"I'll tell you, practicing and playing golf is a lot better than handling divorce cases."

> Terry Dill, attorney who is now on the Senior Tour

"Fifty years."

> Dale Douglass, asked how long it took him to prepare for the Senior Tour

"It would be like leaving a gold mine for a salt mine. It is really tough out there on this tour."

> Stan Dudas, on not leaving his job as a club pro at the Atlantic City Resort to play on the Senior Tour

"I want to be on the senior trout fisherman's tour."

> *Nick Faldo, at age 36, when asked if he planned to enter the Senior Tour in 14 years*

"I went to bed and I was old and washed up. I woke up a rookie. What could be better?"

> *Raymond Floyd, on turning 50 and qualifying for the Senior Tour*

"The King Tut show of antiquities."

> *Herb Graffis, golf writer, when the idea of a senior tour was proposed*

"These old guys are a lot nicer than those kids on the regular tour. I thank them every Sunday night."

> *Don January, on being one of the big winners on the Senior Tour*

"My friends say I ought to do one of those Geritol ads."

> *Don January, on playing in the Senior Tour*

"Combination rest home and gold mine."

> *Dan Jenkins, describing the Senior Tour*

"Senior golf spreads the myth that age allows you to play life from the front tees."

> *Bernie Lincicome, Chicago Tribune sportswriter*

"Never realized how beautiful golf courses really were until I started seeing them with clear eyes. I could have blown my whole career. I did blow my whole career, my first one. But this is the second chance."

> *Larry Mowry, a former pro golfer and recovering alcoholic, who qualified to play on the Senior Tour*

"I don't see Norman and Ballesteros and Faldo out there."

> *Jack Nicklaus, on Gary Player saying that winning the 1990 Senior PGA should qualify as a major*

"The older we get, the further we say we used to hit it and the more we used to hit it out of sight."

> *Phil Rodgers*

"If I could have putted like this years ago, I'd own a jet instead of a Toyota."

Chi Chi Rodriguez, on his play on the Senior Tour

"Most people at age 55 who want to play golf have to join a nice country club or go to Maui. We do both and get paid for it."

Chi Chi Rodriguez, on the joy of the Senior Tour

"When Lee and Jack win, it is good for golf. When I win, it is better."

Chi Chi Rodriguez

"Then Lee Trevino and Jack Nicklaus come in. I'll caddie for Jack."

Chi Chi Rodriguez, after saying he had three good years left on the Senior Tour

"It's like getting divorced and getting remarried the same morning."

Jay Sigel, on turning 50 and giving up his amateur status to play on the Senior Tour

"It's a grind trying to beat 60-year-old kids out there."

Sam Snead, on why he stopped playing on the Senior Tour at age 77

"One of the nice things about the Senior Tour is that we can take a cart and cooler. If your game is not going well, you can always have a picnic."

Lee Trevino

"Why play with the flat-bellies when you can play with the round-bellies?"

Lee Trevino, on joining the Senior Tour

"I knew I was on the wrong tour when I tried to bum a cigarette in the locker room at the 1987 U.S. Open. . . . There were 25 pros in the locker room and none of 'em smoked. I knew my time had gone by."

Lee Trevino, on wanting to join the Senior Tour

"We play a completely different game out here. We don't care much about blue blazers and neckties. It's the numbers, pal."

Lee Trevino, to Jay Sigel, who was just joining the Senior Tour

"He'll be tougher than a 50-cent steak."
> *Lee Trevino, on Raymond Floyd join-*
> *ing the Senior Tour*

"Growing old is mandatory. Growing up is optional."
> *Tom Wargo, stating the philosophy of*
> *the Senior Tour*

SENIOR, SENIOR TOUR

"In 30 years, we're going to be in our 90s. We're going to play three-hole tournaments for $900,000 and the one who remembers his score wins."
> *Bob Bruce*

"I never quit a golf course in my life. But I never got involved in 19th-hole guzzling in the clubhouse, either."
> *Chick Evans, at age 80, on qualifying*
> *for every U.S. Amateur Championship*
> *for 55 years*

"I'm waiting for the Senile Skins Games."
> *Bob Hope, on golfing at age 86*

"I'll shoot my age if I have to live to be 105."
Bob Hope

"I hope that when I see Jones I'll tell him about it."
Gene Sarazen, on receiving the USGA
Bobby Jones Award at the age of 90

"I told Hord [Masters Chairman] I was getting too old to play, but he kept saying, 'Gene, they don't want to see you play; they just want to see if you're still alive.'"
Gene Sarazen, on being an honorary
player at the Masters at the age of 90

"I play by memory: If somebody tells me to hit the ball 150 yards, I hit it 150 yards."
Sam Snead, on barely being able to
see a golf ball

"The old fans root for me, but the kids don't know me. To them I'm some sort of prehistoric thing. If you don't stay before the public by winning all the time, you're a bum."
Sam Snead

SHORT GAME

"Bob has a beautiful short game. Unfortunately, it's off the tee."

Jimmy Demaret, on Bob Hope

JOEY SINDELAR

"I'm basically a par—eagle—double bogey player."
Joey Sindelar, self-description

SKINS GAMES

"I sent Gary a telegram recently. I asked him if he turned over a new leaf."

Tom Watson, on accusing Gary Player of illegally uncovering a ball from a leaf during the Skins Game tournament

SLICES

===

"When a pro hits it to the right, it's called a fade. When an amateur hits it to the right, it's called a slice."

Peter Jacobsen

"I'm not saying my golf game went bad, but if I grew tomatoes, they'd come up sliced."

Lee Trevino

SLOW PLAY

===

"You start your soft-boiled eggs by the time he's ready."

Johnny Miller, on Nick Faldo's methodical play

"If you want to help yourself and the game, don't play slowly. Your concentration wanders."

Gene Sarazen

"We're going to run into the Johnny Carson show if something isn't done about slow play."

Lee Trevino

"I've seen turtles move faster than Bernhard."

Lanny Wadkins, on Bernhard Langer's slow play

SLUMPS

"Knock hell out of them. They'll land somewhere."

Stewart Maiden, to Bobby Jones when Jones was in a slump

"You feel the ball is coming out of the popcorn popper."

Johnny Miller, on playing badly

J. C. SNEAD

"He was so ugly as a kid that his parents tied pork chops around his neck so that the dog would play with him."

Lee Trevino

SAM SNEAD

"Walter Hagen is the first man to make a million dollars in golf and spend it. Snead is the first to make a million and save two."

Fred Corcoran, promoter, on the famous stinginess of Snead

"Sam is so loose that if you cut his wrist, 3 In 1 oil would come out."

Gardner Dickinson

"Of course, he's still got it."

Dave Marr, on Snead getting only $500 for winning the British Open in 1946

"The old superstition says breaking a mirror brings seven years' bad luck. Well, Sam feels the same way about a dollar bill."

Doug Sanders

"If you could get the digging rights to Sam's backyard, you'd never have to work again in your life."

Doug Sanders

"Sam Snead has the greatest swing in the history of golf."

Gene Sarazen

"Is that right? How long are decades nowadays?"

Sam Snead, on winning a tournament in the 1980s and being told he hadn't won any other tournaments in decades

"Like classic plays and symphonies, Sam Snead doesn't just belong to a generation. His mark will be left on golf into eternity."

Peter Thomson

SOUTHERN COMFORT

"If they [Southern people] know you are working at home, they think nothing of walking right in for coffee. But they wouldn't dream of interrupting you at golf."

Harper Lee

SPLENDOR IN THE GREEN

"I put down a dime to mark my ball and it slid all the way to the green."

> *Gay Brewer, on the fast greens at a senior tournament*

"It wasn't bad, but we had to use contemporary greens."

> *Jim Gantner, former major league baseball player*

"You can't putt on putty. I've got a lawn mower back in Texas. I'll send it over."

> Ben Hogan, on the Scottish greens at the 1953 British Open

"I read the greens in Spanish, but putt in English."

> Chi Chi Rodriguez, on his putting problems

SPORTSMANSHIP

"You might as well praise a man for not robbing a bank."

> Bobby Jones, on penalizing himself a stroke that cost him a tournament

CRAIG STADLER

"Craig Stadler has made the athletic world safe for Twinkies and Moon Pies and jogging shoes that you wear only to jog to the refrigerator."

> Scott Ostler, on the heavyset Stadler

JAN STEPHENSON

"If I had legs like that, I'd pose that way too. Don't they have a Miss Piggy category?"

> *JoAnne Carner, defending Jan Stephenson's poses in a magazine*

FRANK STRANAHAN

"He must brush with Sani-Flush."

> *Jimmy Demaret, on Stranahan, who was known for his smile and good looks*

STREAKS

"You stay here all year just to catch that four or five weeks when everything comes together."

> *Ken Green*

"No one has ever conquered this game. One week out there and you are God; next time you are the devil."

Juli Inkster

"How can there be 10-shot differences from one day to the next? I think that's just the nature of this stupid game."

Tom Kite, on shooting a 64 after having shot a 74 the previous day

"One minute it's fear and loathing, but hit a couple of good shots, and you're on top of the world."

Jack Nicholson

"You need a fantastic memory in this game to remember the great shots and a very short memory to forget the bad ones."

Mac O'Grady

"It was one of those days you dream about. Every hole seemed to be six inches wide."

Tom Purtzer

"Some people say I play erratic golf. What they mean is I frequently play lousy."

Tom Shaw

"It's kind of like I just took it out of the refrigerator. It's cold in spots, warm in the others."

Tom Watson, on his golf game

STREAKERS

"It was only a naked woman."

Jose-Maria Olazabal, on a streaker at the British Open

SWING SHIFT

"As far as swing and techniques are concerned, I don't know diddly-squat. When I'm playing well, I don't even take aim."

Fred Couples

"If a great golf swing puts you high on the money list, there'd be some of us who would be broke."

Raymond Floyd

"The harder and quicker you swing, the farther you'll hit the ball and the faster you'll be back in the grill having a gin martini."

Lewis Grizzard, offering his swinging tips

"There is nothing natural about the golf swing."

Ben Hogan, after being told he had a natural swing

"Sam's always been smart enough to know that the surest way to ruin his swing would be to start getting too complex about it. He's kept his thinking simple."

Cary Middlecoff, on Sam Snead's swing

"My swing is so bad I look like a caveman killing his lunch."

Lee Trevino

"When I used to see him come to the clubhouse in the morning wearing a tuxedo, I knew we were in for a bad day."

Leggy Ahern, Walter Hagen's longtime caddie

"I've quit drinking. But don't tell anybody. I don't want to ruin my image."

Raymond Floyd

"Like the greatest party of all time—coast-to-coast golf, good money, and good times."

Roger Maltbie, on life on the Pro Tour

"I must confess that I have no halo around my head. As a matter of fact, I don't even know how to spell halo."

Doug Sanders

"I don't know how much wine we drank, but we had to empty the trash twice just to get rid of the corks."

Doug Sanders, on a wild Tour party

"I was just coming in this morning when he was getting up. Man, a guy can get too much rest."

> *Lee Trevino, on partying all night and then playing Bob Menne in a playoff that day*

TEARS OF JOY

"No problem. I just think of my golf game."

> *Arnold Palmer, on his having to cry to give his contacts proper lubrication*

TEMPER, TEMPER

"They throw their clubs backwards, and that's wrong. You should always throw a club ahead of you so that you don't have to walk any extra distance to get it."

> *Tommy Bolt, on the temper tantrums of modern players*

"Because that's all you have left in the bag. Except for the putter. And it sure ain't a putter."

> *Tommy Bolt's caddie, after Bolt said, "A 6-iron? It's 225 yards. What in the world makes you think it's a 6-iron?"*

"Some players would complain if they were playing on Dolly Parton's bedspread."

> *Jimmy Demaret*

"He was the most even-tempered man I ever met. He was mad all the time."

> *Jimmy Demaret, on golfer Clayton Heafner*

"I was trying to add a little color. Unfortunately, what I added was off-color."

> *Lori Garbacz, professional golfer, fined for shouting an obscenity on ESPN*

"I don't play well enough to be allowed to throw my clubs."

> *Lou Holtz*

"How could I not like Craig? He's the best thing that ever happened to me. He makes me look good."

> *Tom Weiskopf, on Craig Stadler's temper*

THERAPY

"I'd play every day if I could. It's cheaper than a shrink and there are no telephones on my golf cart."

> *Brent Musburger*

"I'm a golfaholic, no question about that. Counseling wouldn't help me. They'd have to put me in prison, and then I'd talk the warden into building a hole or two and teach him how to play."

> *Lee Trevino*

"A hundred and twenty years."

> *Sandy Lyle, asked the difference between winning the TPC and winning the British Open*

"If you birdie the 18th, do you win a free game?"

> *John Mahaffey, asserting that the 18th hole at the TPC at Sawgrass has as many obstacles as a miniature golf course*

"I was just trying to beat Pete Dye today, and I believe I got him."

> *Jerry Pate, on shooting a 67 to win the 1982 TPC golf course designed by Pete Dye*

"They messed up a good swamp."

> *J. C. Snead, on the TPC in Florida*

"This course is 90 percent horse manure and 10 percent luck."

J. C. Snead, on a TPC course designed by Pete Dye

TOURNAMENT TIME

"A tournament is never won until it's lost. And it's never lost until it's won."

Bruce Crampton

"Some players today play two or three tournaments, get tired, and then take a couple of weeks off. I couldn't wait to get to the next tournament. If they're tired, they should go to bed early."

Ben Hogan

"There are two kinds of golf—golf and tournament golf."

Bobby Jones

"I rank this event just behind the Masters at Augusta."

Larry Nelson, on winning the Dunlop Open in Japan

"If I'd win every week, they'd cancel the Tour."

> *Lee Trevino, on missing the cut in a*
> *tournament*

"One under a tree, one under a bush, one under the water."

> *Lee Trevino, explaining how he was*
> *one under during a tournament*

LEE TREVINO

"More people show up to watch Lee Trevino change shoes than watch me tee off."

> *Orville Moody*

"It's like you wind him up and when he hits the course his mouth starts going until he goes back to his room. Then he stops completely."

> *Jack Nicklaus, on the personality of*
> *Trevino*

"If he didn't have an Adam's apple, he'd have no shape at all."

> *Gary Player*

"We have three tours. The Senior Tour, the Super-Senior Tour, and the Lee Trevino Tour."
Chi Chi Rodriguez

"Trevino is in a league by himself. We don't even count him. We figure when you come in second, you're a winner."
Chi Chi Rodriguez, on the Senior Tour

"If conversation was fertilizer, Trevino would be up to his neck in grass all the time."
Larry Ziegler

U.S. OPEN

"The Blast Furnace Open."
Tommy Bolt, on the 1958 Open in Tulsa, Oklahoma, played in incredible heat

"If I ever win again, you can bet the tournament is in trouble. And if I ever win the U.S. Open, they'll probably cancel golf."

> *Ron Cerrudo, journeyman golfer who won several tournaments in 1972*

"An examination of golf. It might be the toughest, fairest test. It calls for tough, honest golf shots."

> *Ben Crenshaw, on Winged Foot, home of the 1984 U.S. Open*

"It's like playing in a straightjacket. They just lay you up on the rack and twist on both ends."

> *Ben Crenshaw, on the pressure of playing in the U.S. Open*

"There's no place you can practice for those greens except for maybe the bathtub if I putt toward the drain."

> *Jim Gallagher, Jr., on the greens at Oakmont, home of the 1994 Open*

"Fourteen strokes."

> *Hubert Green, asked the difference between shooting 81 on the first day of the Open and 67 on the second day*

"Prestige is fine, but a little money won't hurt."

> *Walter Hagen, on receiving a small purse for winning the Open*

"Why don't they give the cows their pasture back?"

> *Dave Hill, on Hazeltine (Chaska, Minnesota), the site of 1970 U.S. Open*

"On this course, a monkey is as good as a man."

> *Dave Hill, on the Hazeltine*

"I'm glad I brought this monster to its knees."

> *Ben Hogan, on shooting a 67 to win the 1951 U.S. Open*

"If your husband had to play this course for a living, you'd be in the poorhouse."

> *Ben Hogan, to the wife of Robert Trent Jones, on the Oakland Hills golf course that Jones designed and where Hogan won the 1951 Open*

"Shoot a lower score than everybody else."

> *Ben Hogan, asked the secret of winning the U.S. Open*

"I felt like a lawn mower that just wouldn't turn over."

> *Peter Jacobsen, on shooting a 76-70-76 in the last three rounds of the Open in 1988*

"The Masters Tournament is fun. The Open is work."

> *Tony Lema*

"My kid's got a big Little League tournament that weekend."

> *Bruce Lietzke asked if he was going to play in the 1992 Open*

"Playing in the U.S. Open is like tippy-toeing through hell."

> *Jerry McGee*

"Nobody wins the Open. It wins you."

> *Cary Middlecoff*

"Like unhitching a horse from a plow and winning the Derby."

> *Jim Murray, on Orville Moody's improbable win at the 1969 Open*

"At that time I was too young and not smart enough to be afraid of Arnold."

> *Jack Nicklaus, on beating Palmer in a playoff to win the 1962 Open*

"If I had been able to beat that strong, young dude in the tournament, I might have held him off for another five years. . . . I let the Bear out of his cage."

> *Arnold Palmer, on losing to Nicklaus in the 1962 Open playoff*

"There are so many doglegs here, Lassie must have designed the course."

> *Bob Rosburg, on Hazeltine, the site of 1970 Open*

"My Open was kind of like a sandwich. But I sure as hell didn't like the meat."

> *Mason Rudolph, on his score of 71-80-86-71 in the 1972 Open*

"I'm disappointed to lose the U.S. Open two days in a row."

> *Scott Simpson, on blowing a two-shot lead in the fourth round and then losing in a playoff to Payne Stewart at the 1991 Open*

"You not only have to be good, but you also have to have two horseshoes up your rear end. You've got to be lucky to win the U.S. Open."

Sam Snead

"Those cotton-pickin' greens look like someone's been out there hoein' corn."

Sam Snead, on not making the cut at the 1975 Open

"No, I haven't called my wife, but if I don't have the $30,000 check there by Wednesday, she'll call me."

Lee Trevino, after winning the 1968 Open

"Buy the Alamo and give it back to the Mexicans."

Lee Trevino, on what he would do with the money from the 1968 Open

"A lot of zeros, with the one number in front."

Lee Trevino, asked how much winning the 1968 Open meant to him

"I played the tour in 1967 and told jokes and nobody laughed. Then I won the Open the next year, told the same jokes, and everybody laughed like hell."

Lee Trevino

"Let him go! Let the big dog eat."

Lee Trevino, on Jack Nicklaus winning the Open after a long slump

"It's surrounded by water on three sides."

Roger Twibell, commentator, describing the 16th hole at Hazeltine during the Open

"I am sure I could go out now and do better by kicking the ball around with my boot."

Harry Vardon, on shooting a 42 on the back nine to lose the 1920 Open by a stroke

"My God, I've won the Open."

Ken Venturi, on winning the 1964 Open after being overcome by the heat

"The suit is so stiff. I can't do this with two hands but I'm going to try a little sand trap shot here."

> *Alan Shepard, astronaut, preparing to shoot on the moon's surface.*

WATER

"Now, when I hit one in the water, the fish will know who to send it back to."

> *Bob Hope, on getting 90 golf balls as a birthday gift that said, "Happy Birthday, Bob"*

"The difference between a sand bunker and water is the difference between a car crash and an airplane crash. You have a chance of recovering from a car crash."

> *Bobby Jones*

"Which one, the Atlantic or the Pacific?"

> *Chi Chi Rodriguez's caddie, after Rodriguez asked him at a tournament in California if he thought his putt would bend to the ocean*

"I didn't hit any spectators. I did get one bass, though."

> *Fuzzy Zoeller, on hitting a lake during a match*

TOM WATSON

"We're the fourth franchise here—behind the Royals, the Chiefs, and Tom Watson."

> *Cotton Fitzsimmons, former coach of the then Kansas City Kings NBA franchise*

"Maybe I should get into a fistfight with Jack Nicklaus on the 18th green."

> *Tom Watson, on creating some controversy in golf*

"You can play golf on Christmas afternoon."

> *Mark Calcavecchia, on the best part about moving from Nebraska to Florida*

"No, that's management. I'm in sales."

> *Reverend John Durkin, asked if he was responsible for perfect weather at a golf tournament*

"A day when I don't have wet socks."

> *Nick Faldo, asked what weather he was hoping for on the final day of the Masters after three days of rain*

"I'm glad we don't have to play in the shade."

> *Bobby Jones, after being told it was 105 degrees in the shade*

"Fate and nothing else beat Harry Vardon that day."

> *O. B. Keeler, on Vardon having a six-stroke lead with seven holes to play in the U.S. Open and losing the lead because of gale-force winds*

"I play in the low 80s. If it's any hotter than that, I won't play."

> *Joe E. Lewis, comedian*

"Hey, Jack. What do you call that—the Gale Mary?"

> *Jim McCone, to Jack Nicklaus, who was in prayer position because of bad weather at the Bing Crosby Pro-Am*

"That Mark Spitz isn't so hot. He never swam 18 holes."

> *Jerry McGee, on bad weather during the 1972 golf season, the year Spitz won seven gold medals in the Olympics*

"I played as much golf as I could in North Dakota, but summer up there is pretty short. It usually falls on Tuesday."

> *Mike Morley, pro golfer from North Dakota*

"It looks like the sequel to *A River Runs Through It*."

> *Chris Perry, on a rain delay at the Monterey Open*

"I wouldn't follow Farrah Fawcett around out here today."

> *Chi Chi Rodriguez, on awful weather at the 1982 Masters*

"The winds were blowing 50 mph and gusting to 70. I hit a par 3 with my hat."

> *Chi Chi Rodriguez, on the winds in Scotland*

"Instead of a bar call, he should have used a premium brand."

> *Payne Stewart, on Jack Nicklaus putting a glass of gin by a grave site near his golf course in Muirfield Village in a vain attempt to ward off bad weather*

"I call that my spring training. I'm not a cold-weather player."

> *Lee Trevino, on not playing well in some spring tournaments*

"I don't want that thing in my hand if lightning hits. The Man up there knows I've been a bad boy."

> *Lee Trevino, on throwing his club to the ground during a thunderstorm delay at a tournament*

"My whole life flashed before me—I couldn't believe I had been that bad."

> *Lee Trevino, on being hit by lightning*

WEDDED BLISS

"We were happily married for eight months. Unfortunately, we were married for four and a half years."
Nick Faldo

"Golf is tougher than my first wife."
Ken Green

"The only place I can find him is on the sports pages."

> *Edna Hagen, wife of Walter Hagen*

"If it weren't for the money, I'd retire and go caddie for my wife."

> Ray Knight, former major league baseball player and husband of Nancy Lopez

"My wife thinks 'don't hold back' means to keep spending money."

> Larry Laoretti, Senior Tour golfer

"This is a honeydew day. That is when you get a day off and the wife says, 'Honey, do this' and 'Honey do that' around the house."

> Jim Lemon, former major league manager, on wanting desperately to play golf on his day off instead of doing chores

"Most country clubs exclude the wrong kind of people, such as me. But I hold out the hope that somewhere there's a club that bars first wives."

> P. J. O'Rourke

"My wife always said she wanted to marry a millionaire. Well, she married a millionaire. I used to be a multimillionaire."

> Chi Chi Rodriguez

"I hate to bother you, madam, when you're so comfortable. But would you move, please? I have a lot of alimony to pay."

> *Doug Sanders, on a woman blocking*
> *his backswing*

"I didn't even have to change the names on the towels."

> *Lee Trevino, on getting married to a*
> *woman named Claudia after being di-*
> *vorced from a woman of the same*
> *name*

"It was a friendly divorce. She left me the piano and the lawn mower; I couldn't play either one."

> *Lee Trevino*

WEDGE SHOT

"A bird flying to the firmaments outlined against an incandescent sky, begging to fall, sashaying gently back to the earth."

> *Mac O'Grady, on his wedge shot*

"I'm not very good with a gun, but I'm hot with a wedge."

> *Anne-Marie Palli, on killing a duck with her wedge while it was flying across the course*

"Dear God, don't let me chili-dip this. Put it in the bunker if you want. Maybe I can hole it from the bunker."

> *Chi Chi Rodriguez, on a wedge shot*

WEIGHTY ISSUES

"He has won more titles at more weight than Sugar Ray Leonard."

> *John Brodie, on Billy Casper*

"Like a lot of fellows around here, I have a furniture problem. My chest has fallen into my drawers."

> *Billy Casper, on the Senior Tour players*

"Ed, you were a victim of circumference."
>*Jimmy Demaret, on Ed "Porky" Oliver*
>*losing a playoff*

"One guy dressed like an NFL team; the other guy dressed like three NFL teams."
>*Dan Jenkins, on heavyset Chris Patton*
>*golfing with Payne Stewart*

"My idea of a diet is, if it tastes good, spit it out."
>*Roger Maltbie*

"It takes a lot of guts to play this game, and by looking at Billy Casper, you can tell he certainly has a lot of guts."
>*Gary Player*

"You can look at my physique and see I'm always hungry."
>*Mike Reid, 5'11", 150 pounds, asked if*
>*he was hungry for his first major*
>*championship*

"When the Lord gave us bodies, he skipped Gardner and left him with only a hat and ears."

> *Don Rickles, on the very skinny Gardner Dickinson*

"The best diet I know is pride in yourself. If I gain an inch on my waist, I have to send 200 pairs of slacks out for alterations."

> *Doug Sanders*

"Yes, I had trouble keeping my shirttail in. And on a wet course, it's also harder to get my stomach out of the way of my club."

> *Bates Shaw, 400-pound golfer, on the disadvantages of playing golf at his weight*

"I'm going to stop drinking 30 beers a day."

> *Craig Stadler, on how he was going to lose 35 pounds*

"I think it's funny that almost all the sportswriters who are always asking why Craig doesn't lose weight are heavier than he is."

> *Sue Stadler, wife of Craig*

"They claim red meat is bad for you. But I never saw a sick-looking tiger."

Chi Chi Rodriguez

"I look at the animals. The alligator sleeps almost all the time. The turtle, when it moves, moves very very slowly. You know why? The turtle and the alligator, they live longer than any other animal."

Chi Chi Rodriguez, on the importance of taking things slowly

"I'd better cut this out. These sea lions are beginning to understand me."

Lee Trevino, on barking at sea lions at the seventh hole of Pebble Beach

"I was trying to pull it back between barks, but he got me on the backswing."

Lee Trevino, on a barking dog breaking his concentration during a shot

"It's not whether you win or lose—but whether I win or lose."

Sandy Lyle

"The longer you play, the better chance the better player has of winning."

Jack Nicklaus

"We must always be humble in victory and cocky in losing."

Chi Chi Rodriguez

"Just figure out a way to get it in the hole, no matter what it looks like."

Lee Trevino

"I just want to win tournaments, whether it's the Screen Door Open or the Canadian Bacon Open."

Lee Trevino

"When you're young, you always say it's inevitable. You're going to win. But when you're old, the inevitable is over with."

> Lee Trevino

WOOD

"When that baby goes and I have to put it to sleep, it'll be a sad day."

> *Amy Alcott, on carrying the same 7-wood for years*

"I'm the best furniture maker in the world. No one hits the wood clubs like I do."

> Lee Trevino

WOODS

"I'm hitting the woods just great, but I'm having a terrible time getting out of them."

> *Harry Toscano*

"What's over there? A nudist colony?"

> *Lee Trevino, on playing with three partners who all hit their balls into the woods*

"I didn't even bother to go look for the first ball. I would have gotten scratches all over my back and I would have had to explain that to my wife."

> *Lee Trevino, on hitting a ball into the woods at the British Open*

WORLD TOUR

"Wayne Grady claims it's cold beer and hot meat pies."

> *Ian Baker-Finch, on why there are so many good golfers coming from Australia*

"About six or seven. Spanish, Argentine, Cuban, Mexican . . ."

> *Seve Ballesteros, asked how many languages he speaks*

"There are European players here from all over the world."

> Mary Bryan, TV commentator, on the Oldsmobile Classic

"This may be embarrassing. I've played in Japan. Is that anywhere near Asia?"

> Fred Couples, asked if he ever played in Asia

"I think the opportunities are vast off the course as well as on it. Besides, I've insulted everyone in Europe."

> David Feherty, golfer from Ireland, on playing exclusively in the United States

"I was a bad tenor. Really bad. And there is nothing worse than a bad Irish tenor. The world is full of them."

> David Feherty

"If they ever found me over there again, they'd know I died and somebody sent my body to the wrong place."

> Dave Hill, on his hatred of Great Britain

"We borrowed golf from Scotland as we borrowed whiskey. Not because it is Scottish, but because it is good."

> *Horace Hutchinson, first Englishman to win the British Amateur Championship*

"It's hard by Yaddlethorpe, Mablethorpe, Cleethorpes, and, of course Thorpe."

> *Tony Jacklin, on his hometown of Scunthorpe, Great Britain*

"I'll probably be hearin' from the bloomin' Queen herself."

> *Tony Jacklin, after winning his first American tournament at age 23 (he did meet the Queen)*

"I don't think Pebble Beach will ever be sold to foreign investors. That would be un-American."
Dave Marr

"I love it here in the United States. In Japan, I have no privacy. In the States, I can have a hole in my jeans and nobody will notice."

> *Ayako Okamato, player on LPGA Tour*

"Someone got my credit-card number. I think it must have been some terrorists. You can't believe some of the countries they called—countries I never heard of."

Jan Stephenson, on receiving a phone bill totaling $136,000

"Columbus went around the world in 1492. That isn't a lot of strokes when you consider the course."

Lee Trevino

IAN WOOSNAM

"Wee Woosie . . . looks as though he ought to be playing miniature golf. Come to think of it, he does play miniature golf."

Mike Downey, Los Angeles Times columnist, on the 5'4" Woosnam

"Wee Woosie is a chatterbox. He makes Lee Trevino look like Marcel Marceau."

Steve Hershey

LEW WORSHAM

"He's the only guy in the world with a built-in bib."
Jimmy Demaret, on Lew Worsham's
large chin

YIPS

"Once you've had 'em, you've got 'em."
Henry Longhurst, golf writer

"The yips is a disease of the nervous system that strikes any golfer who plays in tournament competition long enough."
Sam Snead

KERMIT ZARLEY

"He sounds like a pro from the moon."
Bob Hope

"We investigated, and Zembriski never climbed anything higher than a 7-Eleven."

Lee Trevino, on Zembriski working on skyscrapers before joining the Senior Tour

LARRY ZIEGLER

"Look, if Larry ever dreamed that he beat me, he'd apologize when he woke up."

Lee Trevino, asked if he was concerned because Ziegler was leading him in the first round of a tournament

"With my luck, if I went into the pumpkin business, they'd probably outlaw Halloween."

Larry Ziegler

"I don't think of myself as a celebrity or a superstar. I'm just an ordinary guy who makes his living in a crazy way."

Fuzzy Zoeller

INDEX

*An asterisk appears before names that are referred to in a quote. All other names are the actual sources of a quote.